DEVELOPING AND MANAGING TALENT

A blueprint for business survival

SULTAN KERMALLY

· THOROgOOD

Published by Thorogood
10-12 Rivington Street
London EC2A 3DU

Telephone: 020 7749 4748
Fax: 020 7729 6110
Email: info@thorogood.ws
Web: www.thorogood.ws

Thorogood is a division of
Acorn Magazines Ltd.

A CIP catalogue record for this book is
available from the British Library.

PB: ISBN 1 85418 229 3
HB: ISBN 1 85418 264 1

Cover and book designed by Driftdesign.

Printed in India by Replika Press.

Dedication

This book is dedicated to my wife Laura and my children Zara, Pete, Susan and Jenny, my grandchildren Matthew, Anna and Eve and to all the talented employees in every kind and size of organisation.

Acknowledgements

The subject matter of this book has been inspired by my students and participants of my seminars. My thanks go to them for their 'open' discussion on the subject of talent development.

I thank Angela Spall, Neil Ross and Neil Thomas for their encouragement and for giving me the opportunity to publish this book.

My special thanks go to David Bosdet for allowing me to publish case studies from their management-issues website.

Finally my love and thanks go to my wife Laura, and my children Jenny, Susan, Pete and Zara and my grandchildren Matthew, Anna and Eve for their encouragement and being a part of my life.

About the Author

Sultan Kermally, M.A., B.Sc. (Soc.), LL.B. Ph.D., Dip. Fin. & Accts., Dip. Marketing is a management development consultant and trainer, designing and delivering training courses in Business Strategy, Business Economics, Marketing, Managing People, Managing Performance, Managing Knowledge and Personal Development. He has conducted training in the UK, the Netherlands, Belgium, France, Austria, the Middle East, Hong Kong and Tajikistan.

For several years he has held senior academic positions in Scotland and thereafter senior management positions with Management Centre Europe in Brussels, London Business School and The Economist Intelligence Unit where he held the position of Senior Vice President of The Economist Conferences, Europe.

He has been involved in management education and development for a number of years including distance learning management education courses. He is tutoring MBA modules on Strategy, Managing Knowledge, Strategic Marketing and International Business for the Open University Business School and Durham University Business School.

He is the author of eight management books including his latest book on *Effective Knowledge Management: A Best Practice Blueprint* published by Wiley under the CBI fast-track series, and *The Management Tool Kit* and *Gurus on Marketing* both published by Thorogood.

For consultancy and training assignments he can be contacted by e-mail: Skermally@aol.com

Contents

ONE
Developing talent

'The dominant competitive weapon of the twenty-first century will be the education and skills of the workforce.'

LESTER THUROW

All organisations, small and big, local, national and global need to develop and retain talent in order to do business in a fast-changing market place and market space. Developing talent is essential not only to win but also to sustain competitive advantage.

In some organisations the strategy of developing talent means identifying key employees (the potential stars) who are destined (assuming that their organisations do not 'let them go' in crisis situations) to become key players. For example, one American consulting company, with the help of senior managers, identifies a group of employees who are then gradually groomed to fill in senior rolls such as director or partnership positions.

In other organisations the 'developing talent' strategy applies to all employees so that these employees can achieve new skills in order to enhance their organisational capabilities.

Talent can be categorised functionally as well as generally. For example, some organisations might want to focus on developing marketing talent, or financial talent, or design talent in their organisations while other organisations may want to focus on general talent by encouraging creativity, decision-making or developing leadership skills.

Whether one looks at this subject in a narrow sense or a broader sense, all organisations will agree that developing talent is a 'must' if you want to manage complexity and achieve strategic business objectives.

Why is 'developing talent' important today?

Even though one reads stories of redundancies every day, skills are still relatively in short supply. Multiple skills are needed to do business across different countries and across different cultures. Globalisation (the subject matter of chapter five) has had significant impact on the way we do business today. Labour force is becoming internationally mobile. One of the key principles of the European Union is the creation of free movement of goods, persons, services and capital. Mobility is an important factor of the single market. Since business is becoming increasingly international and the market place becoming increasingly complex and more global, organisations need to have people with appropriate skills but, more importantly, develop these skills to keep abreast of market needs.

> **Skills are still relatively in short supply**

At the 10th European Human Resources Directors' Conference held in Madrid in 2002, Odile Quintin, the Director General of the Commission's employment department, said that in tightening labour markets, there is a risk of companies starting to compete for the most qualified workers.

She said 'If we are to meet the ambitions of the Lisbon Council – to make Europe the most competitive and dynamic knowledge-based economy and society in the world, capable of sustaining growth with more and better jobs, and social cohesion – then we must find ways in which all citizens can participate. We must make use of the potential of all workers. And to meet this challenge investment in human resources, lifelong learning, is the way forward. The success of the companies will depend on their ability to develop the skills of their workforce.'

In addition, in Europe, ageing populations reinforce the importance of not just developing but
also retaining talent within organisations. Such
a strategy is important not only for commercial
for-profit organisations but also for public sector and
not-for-profit organisations. The public sector requires
talented people to deliver cost-effective and efficient public services.

> An ageing population reinforces the importance of not just developing but also retaining talent

The other reason for developing talent is to become a knowledge-driven
organisation. Economies are increasingly based on knowledge. A
growing chunk of production in the modern economy is in the form of
intangibles, based on the use and exploitation of talent rather than physical things. More and more goods, from Mercedes cars to Nike trainers
have increasing amounts of knowledge embedded in them, in the form
of design and innovation. Knowledge is beginning to be recognised as
a key capability if an organisation is to compete effectively in a global
environment. To manage and lever knowledge involves the creation and
transfer of knowledge. Such a process necessarily involves the development of individual talent, however, defined.

The third reason for developing talent is to become an innovative organisation. Innovation is related to the creation, use, sharing and integration
of knowledge.

Finally, doing business in the New Economy demands the recruitment
and development of talent.

Developing talent within the context of managing knowledge

Knowledge is becoming very important in gaining and sustaining competitive advantage. It is now recognised as a key capability if an organisation is to compete effectively in a global market place and within the context of business uncertainty. Managing knowledge enables organisations to anticipate and meet customers' needs, enhance employees' competencies, generate innovations, minimise business risks, reduce costs by not re-inventing wheels and in general bring about business transformation.

Knowledge in an organisation comes in two formats: one is located in employee's heads and is known as tacit knowledge and the other is embedded in processes or codified in written forms (manuals, flow charts etc.). Significant proportions of knowledge in organisations is in a tacit form which means that it is the employees who control knowledge. The big challenge facing any organisation is to manage these employees to use their knowledge for the benefit of their organisations. Organisations themselves have to put processes in place to encourage these employees to not only use but to create and transfer, and in some cases codify, their knowledge to make their organisations knowledge-driven.

> **Significant proportion of knowledge in the organisation is in a tacit form**

Tacit knowledge of an individual can be transferred to tacit knowledge of a team or a group by conversations, dialogue and coaching, mentoring and face-to-face meetings. The creation and transfer of knowledge does not happen by employing clever and talented people. These clever and talented people have to be encouraged to acquire the new talent of transferring knowledge.

These individuals have to be trained in coaching their colleagues and to act as mentors, and they need to acquire the skills of communicating interpersonally. It is imperative for businesses to provide training in the 'personal development' area in order to enable individuals to transfer knowledge.

Once the knowledge is transferred from one individual to another individual or a team, it is still in a form of tacit knowledge. To make such knowledge explicit processes have to be put in place to bring about desired transformation. Technology in this case can be an effective enabler. Documentation, intranet and so on, can be used very effectively to transform tacit knowledge into explicit knowledge. Again, incentives and encouragement have to be given to individuals to participate in such transformation processes. Encouragement would involve training in using technology.

Managing knowledge effectively involves the creation of a thriving environment within the organisation that would facilitate knowledge use, creation and transfer. It is all about developing talent at individual and organisational level.

Once knowledge is codified, existing and new employees use manuals and other documents to make use of the knowledge and by doing so they 'internalise' procedures and practices, and in time develop their own tacit knowledge.

In a knowledge-driven organisation employees culturally have to accept that it is very important from the business point of view to share and create knowledge.

There are some organisations that do not believe in developing talent since they believe the talented staff will only stay for three to five years, so why waste money in development. Organisations with this type of attitude may be successful on a 'hit and run' basis but very soon they will lose talented staff and will find it very difficult to survive. When staff walk away from your organisation you are losing a massive amount of tacit knowledge and thus the human capital of your organisation.

Let me tell you a story

ABC is a leading consulting company based in Brussels. It had twenty partners and one hundred and fifty employees. In 2003 it went through hard times and decided to go through a 'cost-cutting' exercise. It, therefore, decided to make eight partners redundant. One of the partners who was made redundant was the only person in that organisation who had knowledge of off-shore tax. After announcing redundancies the company realised it should not have made that partner redundant.

After three days the company had made an offer to that partner to come back. The partner refused as he was happy to accept the redundancy package and in any case a competitor organisation had made him an offer he could not turn down.

This is a true story of an organisation that lost talent. The question one asks is 'why do good companies do dumb things?'

Knowledge, innovation and development of talent

Innovation plays a very important part in driving the business strategy of every organisation. An organisation does not enjoy sustainable competitive advantage merely by possessing resources and talent. Organisations need to be innovative and ahead of their competitors in order to survive in a competitive environment.

Some of the innovations are the result of new knowledge creation and others are the result of recycled knowledge. Whichever way one looks at it, innovation involves new ways of thinking.

Developing talent to become innovative involves:

- Effective collaboration.
- Team work.

- Generation of ideas.

- Creation of knowledge.

- Sharing of knowledge.

- Integration of different types of knowledge.

Talented individuals working in a failure tolerant organisation would be very creative

Innovation involves taking risks and inevitably, in some cases, brings about failures. Failures should be used as stepping stones toward success. The culture of an organisation has to 'allow' for some degree of failure and put in process ways of learning from failures. This is not an easy thing to do, as for many organisations it is difficult to admit any failure.

Talented individuals working in failure tolerant organisations would be very willing to create, share and integrate knowledge.

Finally, innovation relates not only to products but also to processes and people. Knowledge plus imagination, in an appropriate context, results in innovation.

How to stifle innovation

In her book 'The Change Masters', Rosabeth Moss Kanter[1] highlighted the following ten rules for stifling innovation:

1. Regard any new idea from below with suspicion because it is new and because it is from below.

2. Insist that people who need your approval to act first go through several other levels of management to get their signatures.

3. Ask departments or individuals to challenge and criticise each other's proposals.

4. Express your criticisms freely and withhold your praise.

5. Treat identification of problems as signs of failure, to discourage people from telling you when something in their area is not working.

---

1 Kanter, Rosabeth Moss (1984). 'The Change Masters'. George Allen & Unwin.

6. Control everything very carefully. Make sure people count anything that can be counted frequently.

7. Make decisions to reorganise or change policies in secret and spring them on people unexpectedly.

8. Make sure that requests for information are fully justified and make sure that it is not given out to managers freely. You do not want data to fall into the wrong hands.

9. Assign to lower-level managers, in the name of delegation and participation, responsibility for figuring out how to cut back, lay off, move people around, or otherwise implement threatening decisions you have made – and get them to do it quickly.

10. Above all, never forget that you, the higher-ups, already know everything important about this business.

We are doing business in the new economy

It is said that the world has changed and the future is not what it used to be. The arrival of the New Economy has transformed and is still transforming businesses, small and large. The New Economy demands recruitment and development of talent within an organisation.

Before we analyse whether this is rhetoric or reality, it is important to understand what is meant by the 'New Economy'. Some people associate the New Economy with dotcoms and as a result because of the downfall and failure of many dotcoms they believe there will be a disappearance of the New Economy if we wait long enough and, therefore, one can continue the 'business as usual' strategy.

The world has changed and the future is not what it used to be

The New Economy has very little to do with dotcoms hype as such. The New Economy is an economic phenomenon affecting the whole economy whether one is in e-business or not.

The attributes of the New Economy are as follows:

- The business cycle of 'bust and boom' has been transformed. There is now a somewhat sustained business cycle.

- The growth in many advanced economies, though varying, has been sustained, though there have been some major disruptions such as 11th September, the Iraqi war and other major terrorist activities.

- Inflation rates have been subdued and in many cases remain in single figures in most advanced economies.

- There has been wide spread use of the Internet throughout the world. (In China it is believed that there are about 30 million Internet users today.) The use of the Internet is facilitating doing business at speed and bringing about real-time transactions. The competition now, it is said, is only a click away.

- The nature of the valuation of business is changing as well. Businesses which are not making profits and are not expected to make profits in the short and middle-terms are valued significantly more than their book value.

- The focus in business is now on leveraging intangible assets (human capital and intellectual property) in order to compete effectively.

- Complexity and uncertainty have become the major drivers for business operations.

Because of the use of the Internet and the convergence of the technologies, and because of the transformation of the business models making linear value chains obsolete, skills become obsolete quickly and organisations have to have a talent strategy in order to keep ahead of competition.

Many organisations have not analysed the type of talent required to gain and sustain competitive advantage and are focusing on recruiting and developing technical talent only. This is the wrong talent development strategy.

What type of people should be considered when undertaking recruitment?

The four Es of talent development

Besides determining specialist skills, other factors should also be kept in mind when undertaking recruitment. New recruits should be energetic, enthusiastic, empathetic and entrepreneurial.

1. **Energetic**: To deal with the uncertainty and complexity of the New Economy energy is needed to respond to the speed of change. 'Inertia fatigue' should not be used as an excuse to manage change effectively.

2. **Enthusiastic**: Business models have to be constantly reviewed and changed. Those involved have to maintain their enthusiasm in order to respond to market needs.

3. **Empathetic**: All employers have to get under the skins of their customers, as Tom Peters would put it, and understand their needs. This is more easily said than done. Customers are becoming very discriminating but many organisations still prefer to pay lip service to customer service or service excellence.

To provide service excellence and serve customers properly requires special talent. Not all staff are 'good' at dealing with customers. Customer consideration and care should be the responsibility of all staff.

The new recruits should be energetic, enthusiastic, empathetic and entrepreneurial

4. **Entrepreneurial**: Technical or specialist skills are not enough. Employees in the New Economy have to be innovative and lead the innovation revolution.

In recruiting talent for the New Economy, organisations or agents representing their clients have to be very clear in providing accurate job expectations, in ascertaining that the candidates are willing to upgrade their skills continuously, that the candidates are willing to collaborate with their colleagues in sharing their experience and knowledge, and that they are good at establishing interpersonal relationships.

Hard skills are important but soft skills should play a key part. Soft skills provide the cement of good relationships, trust and open communication. Ignore them or devalue them at your own peril!

Retaining your talented staff

The biggest challenge facing many organisations today is to retain their talented staff. Retaining staff leads to retaining tacit knowledge within the organisation and reducing the costs of recruitment and induction.

. . . .

CASE STUDY

One company's effort to retain staff and capture knowledge

Mrs Campbell worked in the private client department of a leading consultancy organisation. She is a law graduate of ten years standing, is fluent in English, French and German and is very conversant with tax issues relating to France, USA and Germany. She has been very loyal to the company which she joined in 1996.

In 1999 she became pregnant and went on maternity leave with the full intention of returning to her post on a full-time basis. After the birth of her first baby, she, like some other mothers in a similar situation, felt she wanted to spend more time with her child and was considering instead working on a part-time basis. However, she wanted to work on a five-to-nine basis, did not want to be involved directly with outside clients, did not want to do over-time and not be involved with fee-earning situations.

She felt her organisation would not meet her requirements as it had a 'macho-culture'. She therefore resigned giving her reasons. Her boss, on receiving her resignation, immediately phoned her to arrange a meeting and discuss the situation. The boss recognised the value of retaining Mrs. Campbell and discussed a new role for her as 'Knowledge Director'. As a consequence Mrs. Campbell withdrew her resignation and decided to stay with the firm. She works three days a week but makes a contribution equivalent to working five days a week.

The moral of this case is that if you make every effort to retain your talented staff, he or she in return will make an increased contribution to the organisation.

. . . .

It is important to make every effort to retain your staff whose talent constitutes your organisational ability.

Senior managers should take personal responsibility for the loss of staff. Research has shown that a large number of factors contributing to employee retention are within the managers' circle of influence.

Developing talent and building commitment

According to Greenberg and Baron,[2] there are three types of commitment that organisations get from their employees:

1. **Continuous commitment**: which involves employees continuing to work for their organisations because for a variety of reasons they cannot leave. They might find it stressful to change jobs or the change of job may involve relocation.

2. **Normative commitment**: involves employees who continue to work for their organisations because they face pressures from others to do so. It may be that their company has invested in training them or sponsored them to do a course, such as an MBA. They feel obliged to 'stay with the company'.

3. **Affective commitment**: involves employees who continue to work for an organisation because they agree with the corporate strategy and they want to be part of it. Employees take the mission of their organisation on board and they subscribe to corporate values.

Affective commitment is the true type of commitment. When some organisations produce their staff-turnover figures and claim that their employees are happy to stay with them, such belief could be very deceptive if the employees stay with the company because of continuous or normative commitment.

Organisations that develop their people and have an explicit 'talent development strategy' nurture affective commitment.

2 J. Greenberg and Robert A. Baron (2000) 'Behaviour in Organisations'. Prentice Hall

Key points

- Consider managing and developing talent to win and sustain competitive advantage.

- Talent enhances organisational capability.

- Talent enables organisations to manage complexity.

- Talent can be used to create and transfer knowledge.

- Talent is one of the key drivers of innovation.

- The New Economy demands development of talent.

- Build commitment by developing talent.

TWO
Developing talent
– what does this mean?

'It is not enough to say that people are our most important asset; but to believe that people are the customer's most important asset.'

PROFESSOR DAVID ULRICH

In the New Economy human talent has become the most critical source of competitive advantage. The strategy of developing talent has an individual as well as organisational perspective. This book will focus on both these perspectives to understand and gain insight into the meaning of developing talent.

Individual perspective

> Talent is a special aptitude of high mental ability

According to the Pocket Oxford Dictionary of Current English, talent is a special aptitude or faculty of high mental ability. When organisations recruit people they do so based on their requirements and they use various recruitment techniques to select individuals who they think will deliver their organisational or departmental objectives. All these individuals, therefore, possess a special ability and potential for development.

By development, according to the Oxford Dictionary (1988) is meant *'to unfold...; make or become fuller, more elaborate or systematic'*. Developing talent in this context means enhancing an individual's special ability to perform certain tasks and take certain actions. Development necessarily involves learning which can be described as the process by which skills and knowledge are acquired. Education and training promotes learning which in turn facilitates development of talent. The concept of 'developing talent' is very broad ranging; it relates to the individual's capacity to think and act.

Spending money and coming up with various initiatives to develop talent will not produce desired results. The strategy of developing talent must be aligned to corporate strategy. This is where some organisations go wrong. When individuals join organisations they join with certain expectations. They expect organisations to care for them to motivate them and to provide effective leadership. They expect to grow with organisations which means they expect to be given an opportunity to develop their talent.

> The strategy of developing talent must be aligned to corporate strategy

Organisations, in turn, expect these individuals to achieve their business goals and to have an impact on their bottom-lines. Their people selection process should match the skills they are acquiring with their business needs. As the business then grows, organisations, as a matter of strategy, should invest in developing their employees' talent to sustain competitive advantage. Alignment of business and employees' objectives is a MUST in developing a talent strategy.

To send people on training courses is not what developing talent is all about. Some organisations institute training programmes without analysing what their business needs are. For example, sometime ago I was asked to prepare and design a communication training programme for an international company. When I asked why this training was important and how it would be related to business goals, I was told that it was general training for everyone in the organisation because it was good for all parties concerned, and because they had a training budget it seemed best to spend it on general training.

> To send people on training courses is not what developing talent is all about

This particular company had not carried out a training analysis of the needs related to business goals. Though such training would have enhanced the skills of the participants it was not focused enough to address corporate goals.

Not every individual wants to develop his or her talent. Their willingness and enthusiasm depends on the type of organisation they work for, the values of the individual and their want to develop the organisation, and their loyalty to the organisation and the way they perceive the importance of their own development.

The fact that employees have attended training does not necessarily mean that they have developed their talent.

Organisational perspective: Talent and strategy

Organisations develop their strategies and formulate strategic objectives within the context of environmental and competitive environments. Environmentally organisations have to assess change taking place in a sociological, technological, economic and political climate. Their strategies have to be aligned with the changes that would impact their business. In other words, they have to achieve '**strategic fit**' in order to compete effectively. This strategic fit also has to be achieved within the context of the forces operating within their industrial sector. Michael Porter (1980), Professor of Strategy at Harvard Business School, popularised the five forces underlying competition in a particular industry. These forces are the nature and intensity of competition, the bargaining power of suppliers, the bargaining power of buyers, the barriers to entry and availability of substitutes.

For a long time 'strategic fit' was assessed by reference to environmental factors and the nature of the
industry sector. However, in the 1990s the idea of
whether the organisation has a strategic fit or not was
applied to its resources and capabilities. It is believed that
organisational capabilities are deemed to be organisational talent, and
this talent needs to be developed to match the changes taking place in
its competitive climate.

> Organisational
> capabilities
> constitute
> organisational
> talent

ACCORDING TO GRANT [3]

*'During the 1990s, ideas concerning the role of a firm's resources and
capabilities as the principal basis for its strategy and the primary source
of its profitability, coalesced into what has become known as the resource-
based view of the firm. Central to this 'resource-based view' is the idea
that the firm is essentially a pool of resources and capabilities, that these
resources and capabilities are the primary determinants of its strategy.'*

The linkage between resources and capabilities is complex. Hamel and
Prahalad observe that the outstanding capabilities are not always the
result of superior resource endowments. They pose the questions:

- If GM outspends Honda four-to-one on R&D, why are they not the
  undisputed world leader in power trains chassis technology?

- Why has Sony, with a much smaller research budget than Philips,
  produced so many more successful innovations?

---

3 Grant (1991) 'Contemporary Strategy Analysis: Concepts, Techniques, Applications', Blackwell

A firm's resource base has only an indirect link with the capabilities that that firm can generate. The key, according to Hamel and Prahalad, is the firm's ability to leverage resources.[4] Resources can be leveraged in the following ways:

- **Concentrating resources** through the process of converging resources on a few clearly defined and consistent goals; focusing the efforts of each group, department and business unit on individual priorities in a sequential fashion; and targeting those activities that have the biggest impact on customers' perceived value.

- **Accumulating resources** through mining experience in order to achieve faster learning, and borrowing from other firms – accessing their resources and capabilities through alliances, outsourcing arrangements and the like.

- **Complementing resources** involves increasing their effectiveness through linking them with complementary resources and capabilities. This may involve blending product design capabilities with the marketing capabilities needed to communicate these to the market, and balancing to ensure that limited resources and capabilities in one area do not hold back the effectiveness of resources and capabilities in another.

- **Conserving resources** involves utilising resources and capabilities to the fullest by recycling them through different products, markets and product generations, and co-opting resources through collaborative arrangements with other companies.

- **Recovering resources** by increasing the speed with which investments in resources generate cash returns to the firm. A key determinant of resource recovery is new product development cycle time.[5]

. . . .

4 Hamel G and Prahalad, C.K. (1994) 'Competing For the Future'. Harvard Business School Press
5 Grant. Pages 151-152

These special capabilities should be flexible, durable and difficult to imitate

From a human resources point of view leveraging resources to enhance capabilities involves developing, sourcing, integrating and retaining talent within your organisation. This is the only way the organisation can possess distinctive capability. Your competitors can acquire and copy your resources and even acquire the skills you have; what they cannot do, however, is develop the talent in a way that you do it (within the context of business goals) to enhance tacit knowledge.

Organisations priorities have changed in recent years. They now need special capabilities consisting of the sum of individual talents in order to achieve high performance. These special capabilities should be flexible, durable and difficult to imitate. This is where the strategy of developing talent becomes important. Organisations should formulate strategies for developing talent in order to convert and enhance human resources into distinctive capabilities.

In a situation like this recruiting and retaining talent is not enough. Organisational capabilities have to be involved in sustaining strategic fit. This evolution can only be brought about by developing talent at organisational level.

Individual and organisational talent – integrative approach

One cannot talk about individual talent and organisational talent as two distinct entities. Individual and organisational talents are inter-related.

Successful organisations are moving away from training individual employees as something which they have done for a long time in order to enhance and up-grade individual skills to becoming '**learning organisations**'.

Individual and organisational talents are inter-related

The 'guru' of the learning organisation is Peter Senge, the author of 'Fifth Discipline'. He presented the following attributes of a learning organisation:

- The concept of a learning organisation is a vision.
- The learning organisation has to continually expand its capacity to be creative and innovative.
- Learning has to be part of the organisational culture.
- It acquires knowledge and develops talent and leverages them by putting processes in place to encourage and enhance learning.
- It fosters development of employees.
- It has an open communication.

According to Senge, learning organisations are places *'where people continually expand their capacity to create results they truly desire, where new and expansive patterns of thinking are nurtured, where competitive aspirations are set free, and where people are continually learning how to learn together.'* **This can only happen in an organisation that has a distinct strategy to develop their people.**

In a nutshell, learning organisations involve corporate vision, corporate environment that focuses on development of employees' talent that has intellectual (thinking) and pragmatic (doing) dimensions.

Examples of some key *organisational initiatives* to develop employees' talent

Setting S.M.A.R.T. objectives. Many organisations formulate corporate and departmental objectives which are Specific, Measurable, Attainable, Realistic and Time-specific (S.M.A.R.T.). Organisations that believe in developing talent formulate not just specific but **stretch objectives** to provide challenges that contribute to the development of talent. Employees need challenges to develop their potential.

According to Goran Lindhal, who spoke as president and CEO of engineering and technical company ABB, at the Global Human Resource Management Conference in March 1999, **'What motivates people is not reaching a goal, because then the challenge is over, but the highest excitement is pushing hard toward that goal'**.

Associated with stretch objectives, talent development should be an aspect of **performance reviews** that gives recognition of employee's achievement. Without such recognition there will not be an incentive for individuals to develop their talent.

Performance reviews should incorporate not only assessment of current performance in relation to the objectives set, but they should also be used for developmental purposes. At a review session consideration should be given to what employees do now, what they can do, given their talent, and what they would like to do given the opportunity to develop their talent.

Empowering employees also contributes to development of talent. Empowerment is about getting the best out of people. Professor Rosabeth Moss Kanter in her book *'The Change Masters – Corporate Entrepreneurs at Work'* (1983), emphasised the need for people in organisations to work as 'corporate entrepreneurs'. Top management should learn to trust their people and give them the power to be innovative and bring about changes in their organisations.

The concept of empowerment is particularly relevant in the context of talent development. Empowerment is about creating situations where employees share power and assume the responsibility of making decisions for the benefit of organisations and themselves. Empowerment can be looked at from organisational and individual perspectives. Organisations can empower by creating an appropriate culture and climate, and provide appropriate opportunities and effective leadership, but before employees empower themselves they have to be convinced that top management mean business and they are given to develop their talent and realise their potential for mutual benefit.

Top management should learn to trust their people

In the 1980s many organisations like Philips Electronics, Milliken Textiles, 3M and Shell empowered their staff in order to achieve total quality in their products, processes and people. Over the past two decades empowerment has been practised by some organisations to enable decision-making at the coal-face. Now a days empowerment, especially within the context of flat organisations, assumes more importance in enabling employees to develop their talent.

The key success factors of empowerment – how to empower your staff:

- There must be an open and honest information sharing culture within the organisation.

- There should be leadership that can facilitate empowerment.

- There is a need for team building. Individual talent within a team will not bring high performance. Talented individuals have to work as a team.

- Employees should be trained to act as 'entrepreneurs'.

- Employees should understand and internalise corporate strategic objectives.

- The top management should trust their employees.

- Employees, in turn, should give their full commitment to the organisation.

- Organisational culture should 'allow' employees to make mistakes.

- Managers should assume the role of a coach and mentor to help their team achieve desired results.

- Establish parameters.

"The person born with a talent they are meant to use will find their greatest happiness in using it.."

GOETHE

Coaching

Coaching
fosters
individual
development

The learning organisation adopts the concept of coaching in the spirit of developing individual talent. A coach facilitates in bringing out the best performance from the staff. Task-orientated coaching is based on a coach showing how particular tasks should be done. **Coaching in learning organisations is developmentally based rather than being just instructional.** This kind of coaching fosters individual development which then impacts on the performance of that individual in the organisational role he or she occupies.

One way of defining coaching is to look at it as a structured process to develop and harness a person's talent with a view to achieving set objectives.

Coaching involves:

- Explaining the drivers behind performance.
- Taking staff through the stages of how to achieve superior performance.
- Observing and giving feedback.
- Guiding towards improved performance.

Effective coaching is a talent in itself. It involves listening skills, questioning skills, interpersonal skills and the ability to establish rapport. In turn it transforms individuals who then acquire special awareness of what is happening around him or her, and it injects the sense of responsibility.

See people in terms of their future potential, not past or present performance.

What is happening now in practice? Some examples:

1. Investment banks are now targeting ethnic talent. Recently twelve top investment banks including Dresdner Kleinwort, HSBC and Deutsche Bank took part in a programme organised by GTI Specialist Publishers to target undergraduates from ethnic minorities.

2. AstraZeneca Pharmaceuticals strives to achieve the priority of retaining and developing talented employees. AstraZeneca University presents programmes to enable employees to take responsibility of their own talent development.

3. Xerox Canada, drives an inclusive culture which represents, respects and leverages people's differences in enriching their lives and the lives of their customers. According to the information provided by the company, Xerox Canada has a workforce that reflects the Canadian population and their mission is to create an environment where diversity is valued and where all individuals can realise their full potential.

4. According to Honda, the car manufacturers, the heart of their global success is its people. Honda is committed to developing people and turning 'The Power of Dreams' into reality for all those who share their passion for providing customer excitement and excellence in everything they do. The Honda Institute focuses on developing employees' talent.

Key points

- Encourage your staff to continuously develop their talent.

- Organisations need to develop talent to enhance their capabilities.

- Talent development constitutes leveraging resources and achieving 'strategic fit'.

- The learning organisation provides the context within which talent is developed continuously.

- Design appraisal systems that encourage talent development.

- Empower your staff to develop their talent.

- Provide coaching to foster talent development.

THREE
Evolution of talent development strategy

"Be the change you want to see in the world."

MAHATMA GHANDI

The concept of developing talent has entered into management vocabulary only recently. If we go back in management history the focus, as far as achieving superior business performance is concerned, has been on the way physical resources were being used and the way employees were organised to achieve business results. The focus on people as such, began to happen in the early 1920s. This chapter looks at how focusing on people came to happen and how the focus over the years shifted to motivation and leadership.

> Developing talent to manage people effectively involves acquiring insights into behaviours in organisations

Researches began to find out what motivates people at work and how to lead people at work to get superior results, so that managers could be trained to develop their motivational and leadership talent.

Developing talent to manage people effectively involves acquiring insights into behaviours in organisations. It is not just the matter of training managers to develop their talent but also motivate individual employees to develop their talent as well.

Developing talent to motivate employees

For individuals to develop their talent, they need to be motivated. Individuals and organisations would only formulate a talent development strategy if there was going to be a mutual benefit.

A hundred years ago it was believed that employees in general did not want to develop to benefit their organisations. Fredrick W. Taylor, 'guru' of Scientific Management said *'The average working man believes it to be for his best interest of his fellow workmen to go slow instead of going fast.'* His book *'The principles of Scientific Management'* (1911), advocated the development of the science of management with clearly stated rules and laws, scientific selection of training of workers and division of tasks and responsibilities between workers and management. He recommended that there should be a detailed analysis of each job, using the techniques of method study and time study, in order to find the method of working that would bring about the largest average rate of production, the so called 'one best way'.

He also advocated issuing detailed written instructions, training and incentive payments in order to ensure that jobs were performed in the approved manner. He believed that there were large-scale productivity gains to be made among workforces if they were managed properly.

He put forward the following principles:

- Use scientific method in planning each job, formulating clearly stated rules and principles thus avoiding rule-of-thumb methods.
- Workers should be selected on the basis of their suitability, physically and mentally, to give their best efforts.
- Motivation through bonuses and incentives should be used to improve output.
- The task should be divided between planning and implementation.
- The manager should concern himself only with 'exceptions' thus leaving him free to consider broader lines of policy and to study the character and the fitness of the men under him.

(Taylor: *Shop Management,* 1903)

In the first quarter of the twentieth century the quest was for industrial improvement by effectively adopting principles of scientific management. Labour was not considered as a specific factor to focus attention on in order to improve efficiency. It was treated as a general factor of production.

In the second quarter of the twentieth century the attention began to be shifted on people, their aspirations, their development, and their behaviour within the organisation. Among the well-known pioneers in this area were Elton Mayo, Abraham Maslow, Douglas McGregor, Frederick Herzberg and McClelland.

Elton Mayo

Elton Mayo led a group of social scientists and industrial psychologists to study how employees reacted to incentives, rest periods and job design. The Hawthorne study became well known among management students. The study, which lasted for three years, was conducted in the early 1920s at the Hawthorne plant of the Western Electric Company in Illinois, USA.

The study highlighted the following:

- Social and psychological interactions in the workplace have an impact on workers' performance.
- Workers respond to their work environment.
- The existence of informal groups in influencing performance behaviour should not be ignored.
- The style of supervision affected improvement in morale.

The focus on behaviour is important within the context of development of talent because if employees feel 'unhappy' at work they will not be motivated to make efforts to develop their talent.

Abraham Maslow

Among the most influential of the motivational theories emerging from behavioural researches, were those outlined by Abraham Maslow (1908 – 1970). He became associated with hierarchy of needs and workers' motivation. He put forward the theory that people are motivated to satisfy five basic needs:

1. physiological needs (food and shelter)
2. safety needs (security and stability)
3. social needs (affection and acceptance)
4. esteem needs (achievement and self-esteem)
5. self-realisation (self-fulfilment) needs.

> The focus on behaviour is important within the context of development of talent

Motivation to perform depends on the level of needs achieved and fulfilment of these needs affects motivation to perform. Within the context of development of talent, esteem and self-actualisation needs would play an important role in enabling individuals to fulfil their potential. Individuals who have gained self-actualisation needs are working at their peak and they represent the most effective use of their organisation's human resources. Achievement of such needs creates organisational capabilities.

Douglas McGregor

Douglas McGregor (1906 – 1964) put forward a theory relating to the attitude of workers towards work and the style of supervision. If an organisation assumes that people do not like to work, do not want responsibility and will avoid it if they can, then there has to be very tight supervision of such workers. These were theory X assumptions.

On the other hand, if workers like to work and take responsibility, and they perform better with very little supervision then they should be allowed to work with a minimum of supervision and direction. These were theory Y assumptions.

> Individuals who have gained self-actualisation needs are working at their peak

McGreogor proposed theory Y as a realistic view of workers for guiding management thinking. The importance behind theory Y is that organisations can take advantage of the talent development initiatives of their employees.

Employees will contribute to organisational objectives and their own personal objectives, given the opportunity.

Frederick Herzberg

Frederick Herzberg in his book 'Motivation to Work' presented his Motivation-Hygiene theory. He identified several factors which led to job dissatisfaction. These factors, which he called hygiene factors, were salary, company policies and working conditions, for example.

According to his theory, job satisfaction was related to workers' achievement, recognition and taking responsibility for their jobs. He called these factors motivators.

Both hygiene factors and motivators were necessary to improve performance. Herzberg put great emphasis on injecting responsibility into planning and giving workers freedom to control their own work, and on doing the work in whole rather than in units. In other words, he advocated 'job enrichment'.

The job enrichment strategy triggered off the early beginnings of developing individual talent.

Employees will contribute to organisational objectives and their own personal objectives, given the opportunity

David McClelland

David McClelland redefined Maslow's needs approach into achievement needs, affiliation needs and power needs. For more than twenty years McClelland studied human needs and their implications for management. People with achievement needs have to be entrepreneurs, while those with affiliation and power needs are 'integrators' and high performers at top level respectively.

A need for achievement relates to a need to accomplish and demonstrate competence or high talent. **A need for affiliation** is a need for love, belonging and relatedness (establishing close personal relationships). **A need for power** is a need for control over one's own work and the work of others.

An individual's perceived inputs and outputs are compared with their colleagues' inputs and outputs

According to Richard L. Daft, in his book '*Management*', '*McClelland studied managers at AT&T for 16 years and found that those with a high need for power were more likely to follow a path of continued promotion over time. More than half of the employees at the top levels had a high need for power. In contrast, managers with a high need for achievement but a low need for power tended to peak earlier in their careers and at a lower level. The reason is that achievement needs can be met through the task itself, but power needs can be met only by ascending to a level at which a person has the power over others.*'

In the late 1960s and 1970s the focus changed from needs theories to examining how people are motivated and what sustains motivation.

Researchers began to put forward **process theories** which explain how employees select behavioural actions to satisfy their needs. Process theories incorporated Equity theory and Expectancy theory.

According to equity theory, individuals are motivated to maintain fair relationships among themselves and to avoid those relationships that are unfair.

Within the context of developing individual talent, if an individual feels that an organisation takes advantage of their experience and development, and that the efforts they make is rewarded less than other colleagues who do not have as much experience or make as much effort to develop their talent, this will affect individual behaviour.

An individual's perceived inputs and outputs are compared with their colleagues' inputs and outputs.

Under the umbrella of expectancy theories some management theorists put forward the view that whether a person is motivated or not depends on the perception of the outcome of his effort. If the outcome meets his needs then he will be motivated. There is a high link between the efforts an individual puts in to his work and performance.

Expectancy theories had two basic components. They are expectancy and valence components. Expectancy relates to the perception that putting effort into a given task will lead to high performance. For this expectancy to be high, an individual must have the ability to perform and the capacity to develop talent. On the other hand if he believes that no matter how hard he tries to develop his or her talent the organisation will not pay any attention, then he will not make an effort.

Expectancy relates to the perception that successful performance of a task will lead to the desired outcome. Valence is related to the attraction an individual has for an outcome.

If an individual believes that by developing their talent their performance will increase and his or her reward will be commensurate with his or her efforts and the contribution achieved, he or she will be poorly motivated if the rewards have a low valence. It is the value that an individual attaches to the outcome that matters.

Motivation – present day perspective

Many organisations now provide incentives such as stock options to motivate their staff. But the way the stock market has been performing lately (2003) the power of stock options as an incentive has weakened significantly. There is no doubt that finding ways to motivate staff in a recessionary climate and in a situation of uncertainty has been the biggest challenge facing organisations today.

Many surveys and researches have indicated that recognition is very important for employee motivation in a knowledge-based economy.

Organisations have to set stretch goals so achieving these goals means something to employees. Organisations should make an effort to find out what intrinsically motivates their staff. There is always a danger of following 'best practice' elsewhere but every organisation is unique in the type of employees they have.

Recognition is very important for employee motivation in a knowledge based economy

Maslow's theory is still alive today if it can be adapted to take into account the complexity of needs and behaviour. Instead of thinking in hierarchical terms the factors such as physiological needs, social needs and psychological needs should be considered concurrently. These needs exit for every employee. What differentiates one employee from another is the scope and degree of each need. Experts on motivation identify seven critical success factors for an effective recognition programme. They are:

- sincerity;
- fairness;
- timeliness;
- frequency;
- flexibility;
- appropriateness; and
- consistency.

Developing leadership talent

Along with developing talent to gain insights into what motivates people at work, various theories were developing at the same time focusing on developing leadership talent.

For a number of years management theorists have been asking questions on leadership. What makes a person an effective leader? Is a good leader born or trained? What is the best leadership style?

Leadership theories can be categorised into:

a) trait theories

b) behavioural theories

c) contingency theories

d) type theories.

Trait theories

Trait theorists believed that leaders are born. Great leaders had inherent traits such as high intelligence, self confidence and charisma. Effective leaders were born with talent to lead people. Because of various disagreements among management theorists and scholars the search for other explanations of leadership began.

Behaviourist theories

Behaviour theorists believed that leadership is a function of the behaviour of the individual. Leadership behaviour exists on a continuum ranging from authoritarian behaviour on one end of the scale, to laissez-faire on the other.

In 1939 findings were published by some influential researchers from Michigan University which indicated that the authoritarian style stopped initiative and bred hostility; the democratic style promoted better attitude and the laissez-faire style left the group without direction. Leaders may adjust their styles depending on the situation. If, for example, there is time pressure on a leader, or if it takes too long for subordinates to learn or develop their talent, then the leader will tend to use an autocratic style.

At the same time as the Michigan studies, other leadership studies were being conducted by the Bureau of Business Research at Ohio State University, in 1945. The studies picked out two aspects of leadership style which had significance as far as employee performance was concerned. These were:

- **Consideration**: rapport between the leader and his team; trust and concern for his people; and

- **Initiating structure**: the work is organised prescriptively and is done as planned.

Contingency theories

All the theorists so far have emphasised the traits and behaviour of leaders. Fred Fielder in the late 1960s highlighted the role of situational factors. According to Fiedler, leadership was the function of the relationship between the leader and his group, and task orientation. The more directive style worked best in situations where a leader was liked and trusted by his group.

This theory enabled leaders to change their styles depending on the situations they were confronted with.

Other theorists, like Heresy and Blanchard, focused a great deal of attention on the characteristics of employees in determining leadership style. According to them people vary in readiness level. People low in task readiness, because of lack of skill or competence, need a different leadership style to those who are high in readiness level because of their training and experience. The leaders should evaluate subordinates and adopt whichever style is needed.

Another contingency approach to leadership is called path-goal theory. According to this theory the leader's responsibility is to increase subordinates' motivation to attain personal and organisational goals. The leader works with the subordinates to help them identify and learn the behaviours that will lead to successful task accomplishment and organisational rewards.

In spite of various researches throughout the century, there still seems to be a 'leadership vacuum'. The business world has changed and is still changing very dramatically. In chapter four and five we will examine the e-dimension and the process of globalisation respectively. Understanding the context and leading their organisations through major strategic change requires leaders to develop specialist talents to help employees to respond to the changes demanded of them.

One cannot divorce questions of motivation, leadership and developing talent as they are all inter-related. Changes in organisational structures and cultures demands new ways to motivate and lead people to develop their talent.

Because leadership has become such an important issue in the modern business climate, the next chapter is devoted to developing leadership talent and to consider the views of management 'gurus' on leadership.

Key points

- Motivation forms key components of desire to develop talent.

- Needs of individuals and their behaviour play a key role in motivation.

- Various theories have been put forward over the years to find out what factors motivate people at work.

- These theories range from needs theories represented by writers such as Maslow and Herzberg to process theories.

- These theories have made a significant contribution in enabling business executives to manage in practice.

FOUR
The e-dimension

> *"People do not lack strength; they lack will."*
>
> **VICTOR HUGO**

It is said that the world has changed and the future is not what it used to be. The arrival of the new economy is transforming businesses and the war for talent is intensifying.

Whether this is rhetoric or reality it is critical to understand what the new economy is and how the Internet has transformed, and will continue to transform, the way business is conducted in the competitive arena of the twenty-first century.

Some people associate the new economy with the emergence of dotcom organisations and because of the disappearance of numerous dotcoms in the past two years, it is believed that the new economy will also disappear if we wait long enough. However, the new economy has very little to do with dotcom organisations as such. The new economy is an economic phenomenon affecting the whole economy whether you are in an e-business or not.

What are the attributes of the New Economy?

They are:

- The business cycle of boom and bust has been transformed over the past decade. There is now, relatively speaking, a sustained boom cycle though after the tragic events of September 11th this was doubted for a short period.

- The growth rates in many developed countries, though varying, have been sustained.

- There is an increase in productivity and again the resurgence of productivity is sustained. At present there is some concern in relation to the falling productivity in the USA but overall the productivity increase is impacting on our macro-economic environment.

- Inflation rates have been subdued and will continue to be subdued.

- There has been a widespread use of the Internet globally. The Internet is facilitating doing business at speed and bringing about real-time transactions. The competition is now a click away.

- The nature of the valuation of business is changing dramatically. We have now entered the era of knowledge economy which is putting pressure on acquiring, retaining and developing talent.

- Technologies are converging and because of the knowledge economy, skills are becoming rapidly obsolete and a special talent is demanded to provide organisational capability.

The success of e-dimension depends on converting 'e' into **energy** (required to deliver speed), **enthusiasm** (staff have to be enthusiastic to develop their talent), **empathy** (the business has to get under the skin of its customers), **enterprise** (businesses have to build **entrepreneurial** talent) and **evolution** (the business has to evolve its capability to manage change).

Developing talent becomes the most important strategy if organisations have to operate within the context of e-business. To understand the extent to which employees' talent is to be developed on a continuous basis, it is important to understand the attributes of an e-business:

> In recruiting talented individuals, organisations have to be very clear in providing accurate job requirements and in ascertaining that the candidates are willing to upgrade their skills and develop their talent continuously

- e-businesses are on-line;
- they have flexible structures;
- they have to be responsive to customers' needs;
- they need to have an entrepreneurial outlook;
- they operate in the global arena;
- transactions are effected in real-time;
- they are borderless organisations;
- they use the Internet, intranets and extranets as facilitators of business transactions; and, above all,
- they require talented employees.

In recruiting talented individuals, organisations have to be very clear in providing accurate job requirements and in ascertaining that the candidates are willing to upgrade their skills and develop their talent continuously, are willing to collaborate with colleagues within the organisation and share their knowledge, and that they will establish good interpersonal relationships.

Hard skills as well as soft skills are important in all types of business. Soft skills facilitate collaborative culture, trusting relationships and open communications.

Employees nowadays have high expectations of good salaries but at the same time they want to be respected, have their talent recognised and the opportunity to develop this talent further. They also want to establish 'communities of practice' to share their knowledge.

Role of the Internet

The beginning of e-business lays in the origin of the Internet. In the 1990s e-business hit the market as the Internet opened up to commercial traffic. New organisations began to develop based on the use of the Internet to do business, and with that started the mania of dotcoms. However, e-business has also been embraced by the traditional brick-and-mortar organisations like General Electric, Motorola, Unilever, Philips, Pirelli, Wal-Mart, Tesco and so on.

According to Larry Ellison, CEO of Oracle *'In five years' time all companies will be Internet companies… or they won't be companies.'*

When Jack Welch, retired CEO of General Electric was asked where he placed Internet in his business priorities. He answered:

'Where does the Internet rank in my business priorities? It's number 1, 2, 3 and 4.'

The Internet has opened up all kind of possibilities and e-business ranges from product and channel extensions to radical and dramatic departures from traditional business models. The source of energy that will continue to give e-business competitive advantage is the knowledge that exists within the heads of the talented employees. The way talent is used and developed will create knowledge for the organisation.

Development of talent, knowledge and e-learning

Knowledge is increasingly becoming the most intangible asset of every business. Knowledge is created, transferred and used by individuals. Technology is merely a facilitator of knowledge creation and transfer. There are basically two types of knowledge; they are tacit knowledge and explicit knowledge. Tacit knowledge resides in an individual's head. It is personal knowledge and it has a technical as well as cognitive dimension. Explicit knowledge is the knowledge that is codified and embedded and recorded.

Development of talent is about the creation of tacit knowledge. Talented individuals are today's knowledge workers. These workers have experience and training, and they are constantly in need of enhancing their tacit knowledge. Such enhancement comes from coaching, workshops, speaking and sharing experiences with others, and most importantly learning.

The Internet and its variant the intranet are being used to develop individual talent by enabling individuals to share their knowledge via e-channels and by recording their knowledge so that at least some aspects of tacit knowledge are made explicit by recording after action reviews. For example, one project company requires all its employees to record their experience after completion of their projects, and to share this experience via electronic media to those who are interested and require this information so as not to reinvent the wheel when working on subsequent projects.

Some companies have now embarked upon e-learning which makes use of all the advantages of the Internet. It allows content to be current and relevant and employees can develop their talent in their own time, and in the mode they want to choose.

> The Internet and its variant the intranet are being used to develop individual talent

Of course, distance learning courses have been available for a very long time and it has made it possible to acquire education in ones own time. However, e-learning is revolutionary in that it facilitates two way communications between trainers and students.

At Volkswagen UK headquarters, based in Milton Keynes, staff are encouraged to develop their talent by attending a variety of workshops but, in addition, the company has a unique facility for those interested in using e-learning facilities to enhance their skills in performance appraisal, motivation, project management, presentation skills and the like.

Trainingmag.com produce the league table of the organisations (Top 100) that value individuals and their contributions to organisational success by enabling individual's potential. Some 90 percent of the Top 100 companies, according to the website, strategically align personal development plans with overall corporate missions, goals and objectives. (This point was made in chapters one and two.) Aligning personal potential and aspirations to organisational objectives develops organisational capability to compete effectively, and at the same time it motivates individuals to develop their talent.

At Pfizer, Ford Motor Co. and Ernst & Young, for example, employees are able to assess the competencies required to perform tasks at different levels and create their own development plan, and use e-learning to fill in the gaps.

At Booz Allen & Hamilton and The Boeing Co. employees are able to assess information on the competencies required at each stage of their career ladder and map their own development plan.

IBM provides a copious assortment of corporate training programmes. According to trainingmag.com, 'Building on the success of the basic Blue program – a blended initiative for new managers that won three ASTD Excellence in Practice awards in 2000 – IBM launched a similar program for existing managers called Managing@IBM. It is powered by a patent-pending LCMS that uses an expert intelligence agent'.

In order to align corporate objectives with personal objectives and deliver business results, many organisations like Honda, Unipart, Pfizer, Motorola and the like, have formed their own universities and institutes and provide a range of training programmes at different levels to develop the talent of their employees.

AstraZeneca University (UAS) has a web site with access to learning, resources and expertise from other professionals. According to their website, 'Based on the concept of a virtual corporate university, AZU has redefined their approach to deliver, implement and manage training and development at AstraZeneca. The employees are encouraged to self-manage their own professional development.'

The Honda Institute provides services in skills development, product familiarisation, recruitment and assessment, technical training and distance learning using PC technology.

Unipart set up what was one of the first corporate universities in the UK and has been delivering learning through a variety of media ever since. The company had been making extensive use of e-learning for several years, to provide employees with short, snappy pieces of 'just in time' training.

E-learning is becoming very popular but it has some drawbacks:

- Some people do not find time to sit behind a computer and learn all the stuff.
- It lacks a human touch.
- Learning should be, and needs to be, supported with coaching.
- It can be boring and it requires investment in up-to-date resources.

However, employers and employees realise that in a global competitive environment (see chapter five), building talent is imperative and every opportunity has to be taken to do so. According to Strategy+Business website, we now see the emergence of a 'New People Partnership'.

'What exactly is the New People Partnership? Reduced to its simplest terms, the partnership is full implementation of the new realities that exist between the corporation and its employees. Specialist skills are increasingly required by firms, yet these skills are what make employees more mobile in the workplace. Since companies can no longer guarantee lifetime job security, a new quid pro quo is needed. Thus, in the New People Partnership, the company assumes responsibility for investing in the employee and providing work that makes the individual 'employable' in the marketplace. The employee owns his or her career and takes on the burden of building the capabilities that add value to the organisation and insure his or her own marketability. The employee and the company work together to insure that the organisation meets market needs and is successful, since ongoing success provides the context for ongoing employment.'

E-learning is used by some organisations to provide facilities to employees to upgrade their skills and develop their talent in a fast changing business environment. It is said that 'learning has never been so interesting'.

'Information technology will bring mass customisation to learning too....Workers will be able to keep up-to-date on techniques in their field. People anywhere and everywhere will be able to take the best courses taught by the greatest teachers', says Bill Gates writing in 'The Road Ahead'.

CASE STUDY

How Unipart has responded

Learning, knowledge and employee development are at the centre of Unipart's business and cultural vision. It has underpinned a remarkable turnaround from an ailing state-owned parts division into one of Europe's largest distribution, logistics and manufacturing groups. Worldwide it is lauded for its distribution and manufacturing excellence. By 1999 revenues were £1.4 billion with gross profits of £84 million.

John Neill, Unipart's deputy chairman and CEO says, *'Learning has become the platform from which we can see the direction for the future. There is good commercial argument for it – it's a route to competitive advantage and it enhances shareholder value by preventing our peoples' skills from becoming obsolete.'*

To achieve its goals Unipart created one of the world's leading corporate universities – Unipart U having already developed 'bricks & mortar' learning centres at each location, Unipart wanted to reduce the time it took for employees to learn by introducing a 'virtual' learning environment.

THE SOLUTION

Already a long-time user of Lotus Notes and Domino for messaging and calendaring, Unipart used the products and its own Lotus-accredited IT department to create a web site effectively bringing the Unipart U on-line.

Staff can access the Unipart U on-line through their desktops or in the Faculty on the Floor, especially equipped learning centres located 'on-line' in manufacturing and distribution centres. Lotus' e-learning solutions team worked with Unipart to provide the Lotus technology integrated with Path Ware – a learning management software tool now integrated into Lotus; LearningSpace4.

Benefits of e-learning – one specific example:

At a factory, classroom-based training on how to use highly sensitive micrometer equipment was taking an average of six hours. The virtual Unipart U reduced this to just one hour. It has also improved understanding concepts such as continuous improvement, lean production methods and providing outstanding customer service. In the classroom students can sometimes misinterpret meanings or make incorrect assumptions. With on-line learning, students have to understand fully each concept before progressing. In a virtual learning environment students can repeat elements of the course as many times as necessary. 'This approach is much more reliable and students feel better about the learning process. We find this a tremendous benefit', adds Nigriello.

Best practice advice given by Unipart

- Do not be blinded by technology.
- Do not lose sight of the original objectives.
- Align business goals with learning outcomes.
- Create a blended learning environment.
- Manage knowledge effectively.
- Understand an individual's learning style.
- Identify subject area experts.
- Source or develop the most effective learning materials.
- Use technology as a facilitator.

According to John Carroll, Product Manager at Unipart Advanced Learning Systems, 'A key challenge for many organisations will be to shift their focus from a technology-led, e-Learning system, to a broad-based blend of appropriate learning techniques.'

Source and copyright: Unipart website.

Key points

- Talent development can be leveraged by e-learning.

- The Internet is a very powerful medium to facilitate e-learning.

- The Internet and its variant intranets and extranets are being used to develop talent.

- Align corporate objectives with individual aspirations in promoting e-learning.

- E-learning should be used to further personal development.

- If organisations are willing to invest in technology then employees should be willing to invest time to take advantage of e-learning.

FIVE
The global dimension

The term 'globalisation' was coined in the 1980s to mean the economic interdependence of countries. It affects a fundamental transformation of the structures and the nature of international trade. The process of globalisation influences the way we trade, the way we choose our trading partners, the way we decide to upgrade the skills of our workforce and develop their talent, the way we promote creativity and innovation and the way we try to gain insight into various cultures and values. Globalisation, therefore, is an all-embracing concept.

Since 1980 organisations have viewed the world market as a triad comprising the regions of Asia-Pacific, the North Americas and Europe. What globalisation has done is enabling, what is called, 'borderless organisations'. The collapse of communism, the changing political dogmas, privatisation, de-regulation, universal support for market economies and convergence of technologies have all been the main drivers of the globalisation process. It is this process which has prompted some authors to write doomsday books on the subject of 'The Death of Distance', 'The Death of Money' and even 'The Death of Economics'.

Globalisation affects a fundamental transformation of the structures and the nature of international trade

The focus of globalisation from a business perspective is on trade and competitiveness. After the Second World War, twenty-three countries met at Geneva to establish a forum for trade liberalisation. They signed the General Agreement on Tariffs and Trade (GATT), its main objectives being the reduction of tariffs and the promotion of free trade over the years. Between the first and second rounds of GATT talks, approximately 50,000 tariff concessions were negotiated.

> The diffusion of technology and the convergence of technologies will continue to play a key role in accelerating the globalisation process

In 1994, the World Trade Organisation was established to cover trade agreements relating to goods, services, intellectual property and a new dispute-resolution mechanism.

Tariff reductions, subsidies, import licensing and intellectual property protection affect all sizes of business – small, large, national and global.

In order to reinforce the liberalisation of trade various trading blocs such as the North Atlantic Free Trade Association (NAFTA) and the European Union, have come into existence. The European Union, as we know it, was created by the Treaty of Rome which took place in 1957 and consisted of Belgium, the Netherlands, Luxembourg, the Federal Republic of Germany, France and Italy.

In 1992 the European Union began creating the Single Market to facilitate the free movement of goods, services, capital and labour. The European Union also set the goal of achieving a single currency among its members.

The diffusion of technology and the convergence of technologies will continue to play a key role in accelerating the globalisation process. Globalisation has become a reality that, for better or worse, touches our lives in many ways. According to the Financial Times (6, December 1999), *'The global village first conceived by Marshall McLuhan in the 1960s has become a reality for many millions more people exposed to CNN broadcasts, MTV and America on Line'*.

Not everyone is excited about globalisation. Some people feel that many governments have surrendered their power to big businesses. 'Profits rule, not people' as the cliché goes. According to the Economist Newspaper, *'The institutions that in most people's eyes represent the global economy – the IMF, the World Bank and the World Trade Organisation – are reviled far more wildly than they are admired.'*

Why is there an anti-globalisation lobby? First of all, some critics argue that globalisation does not reduce poverty. It creates the world for rich and the world for wretched. Rich countries gain as export creates high paying jobs but importing countries lose out because their jobs are destroyed. Secondly, some countries outsource their production to low-wages countries. This results in sustaining low skills in importing countries and discouraging the development of talent in exporting countries.

Globalisation also creates inequality. Again quoting The Economist of 29 September, 2001, *'In a country such as the United States, the combined action of trade and capital flows is likely to raise the demand for relatively skilled labour and lower the demand for relatively unskilled labour. Some hitherto low-wage workers may succeed in trading up to high-paid jobs, but many others will be left behind in industries where wages are falling. In this scenario, high and average wages may be falling – and that means greater inequality.'*

There are winners and losers as far as globalisation are concerned. However, what is important to consider in the context of developing talent is that globalisation is accompanied by development and convergence of technology. And it is this combination which has caused 'war for talent'.

A country's opportunities to participate in trade and to take advantage of technology are shaped by the skill structure of the labour force. Talent needs to be developed in order to gain benefits from globalisation and diffusion of technology, and at the same time these two forces necessitate a talent development strategy for the organisations that want to gain and sustain competitive advantage. This applies to developed as well as developing countries.

Presiding over the 35th Annual Convocation of the Indian Institute of Foreign Trade, the Minister of State for External Affairs emphasised the importance of the acquisition of new skills and development of employee talent if his country wanted to successfully face new economic challenges triggered of by globalisation and technological development.

> **Talent needs to be developed in order to gain benefits from globalisation and the diffusion of technology**

According to the Caribbean Ministry of Labour, a critical challenge for the country will be the preparation of labour forces to meet the demands of a new international economic order. The government has to ensure that their labour forces are well educated, appropriately trained, flexible and well-informed. Over the next ten years Caribbean countries will face greater economic challenges from the movement of trade liberalisation and economic globalisation.

Richard Heeks and Anne Slamen-Mccann reviewed research literature on job and skill impacts associated with new manufacturing technologies and more globalised production in the East Asian electronics export industry. They focused on East Asian newly industrialising countries, namely, Hong Kong, Singapore, South Korea and Taiwan.

These countries started some years ago to play 'catch up' as far as technological developments were concerned. Current research suggests that the electronics industries of these countries can be said to have 'caught up' though with varying degrees of success.

In a situation like this the countries go through the following 'talent development' stages:

- Initially the firm becomes entirely dependent on imported technology and foreign high level skills. The firm relies on 'experts' from the transnationals to transfer skills.

> **As far as developed countries are concerned, globalisation and technological developments have had significant impact on sourcing skills (talent) in different countries**

- At the next stage the technological dependency begins to decline as it begins to build technological capabilities by developing technological talent. Gradually in the next stage technological talent is developed at a high level to manage latest technology sourced internally as well as externally.

- Throughout all stages a firm maintains commitment to develop talent by promoting training and learning.

As far as developed countries are concerned, globalisation and technological developments have had a significant impact on sourcing skills (talent) in different countries. Texas Instruments' high speed telecommunications chip was conceived by engineers from Ericsson Telephone Co. in Sweden and designed in Nice with software tools the company had developed in Houston. Electrolux has a research laboratory in Finland, a development centre in Sweden and a design group in Italy. Skills and knowledge are now being managed across borders.

Globalisation accompanied with the diffusion of technology creates a shortage of talent. Companies are trying to achieve dual objectives – to keep their costs down and gain and retain appropriate talent. According to one website, Japanese technology leaders such as NEC Corporation, Hitachi Ltd and Fujitsu are scrambling to hire fresh talent in China to cut costs and improve software development as a pool of suitably skilled domestic engineers dries up. Because of a shortage of engineering talent in Japan, these companies are targeting China and India.

Globalisation and the development of specialised talent

Professor Theodore Levitt wrote an article in Harvard Business Review (1983) in which he advised companies to develop standardised high quality world products and market them around the world using standardised advertising, pricing and distribution. According to Levitt, globalisation creates a 'homogeneous global village' and there was no need to develop specialised marketing talent to compete effectively.

Some organisations such as Parker Pen failed following Levitt's advice as it was soon discovered that globalisation does create the need for a specialised marketing talent that was essential to address multi-cultural markets. Companies like Coke and Unilever soon learnt to develop the strategy of 'global localisation' which meant that the marketers had to have a special talent to 'think globally and act locally' in order to respond to similarities and differences in the market place.

To develop global marketing talent requires insight into brand creation and management, product design and positioning, packaging, distribution and customer service.

Globalisation and the 'war for talent' promote and accelerate the movement of people. According to the McKinsey Quarterly, *'In the 1990s, roughly 650,000 people from emerging markets migrated to the United States on professional-employment visas. Over 40 percent of the foreign-born adults in the United States have at least some college education, thereby making that country the epicentre of the global talent drain. Foreign born workers now make up to 20 percent of all employees in the US information technology sector. About 30 percent of the 1998 graduating class of the famed Indian Institute of Technology – a staggering 80 percent of the graduates in computer science – headed for graduate schools or jobs in the United States. Some 80 percent of foreign doctoral students in science and engineering plan to stay there after graduation – up from 50 percent in 1985. Roughly a third of the R & D professionals of developing coun-*

tries have left them to work in the United States, the members of the European Union or Japan.'

What are the implications of such global movement of the labour force?

- Developing countries need technological talent. Brain drain to other countries will deprive these countries of taking advantage of globalisation and technological developments.

- Developing countries have to rely on attracting their nationals from other countries but they cannot offer the incentives offered by developed countries.

- Some countries like Singapore and Thailand, for example, have put in place Reverse Brain Drain projects to attract their nationals back to promote economic growth.

- They may feel there is a danger of developing local talent if they then leave for developed countries.

- Equally, global companies may feel they need to develop expatriate talent in order to compete effectively in a global market place. Unilever, for example, believes that as the company grows globally there is a need for more and more expatriates. The company recruits expatriates internally but they also recruit from the worldwide job market if the internal skills do not exist.

- According to McKinsey consultants, emerging markets can win in the global war for talent by leveraging the talents of their expatriates.

> Globalisation creates not only diversity of market place but also diversity of workforce

The talent drain is not just from developing countries to developed countries but the drain also takes place among developed countries. According to Deloitte and Touché in the UK we are seeing very senior US and mainland European workers take leading roles in high profile companies such as Marks & Spencer.

Globalisation creates not only diversity of market place but also diversity of workforce. Organisations have to make efforts to develop talents of managing diversity within its organisation and manage cross-cultural teams, but also develop awareness of the impact of cultural differences in work-places and values. This aspect of the development of talent becomes imperative if organisations are to have more expatriate staff.

Organisations need to consider talent development strategies geared to create and leverage expatriate talent. IBM and Gillette, for example, have different strategies to create global talent and to accommodate the needs of global workers. Global talent comprises people whose careers are based globally who have worked for an extended period of time in a location or locations outside their home country. Global workers are people who are employed by a global company but are citizens of the country in which they work. Global talent has career aspirations at global level, whereas global workers have career aspirations in relation to their home countries.

Developing talent of women workers

Finally, one must not ignore the talent of women workers. There are now opportunities for women to pursue international careers and organisations should make efforts to encourage development of talent and create more opportunities to leverage this talent.

According to one website *'the softer, feminine skills of women have become valuable in the global market place. Women are naturally caring, nurturing, enhancing and multi-tasking. Add to this their ability for communication and you see people fit to slot into today's demanding, global cooperation.'*

Dr. Hilary Harris, Director of Cranfield University's Centre for Research into Management of Expatriates, believes that women are particularly suited to the global workplace.

How to develop talent: Best practice guidelines

A, B, C of best practice talent development

Globalisation reinforced with convergence and diffusion of technologies has created many challenges for an organisation to develop a multitude of talents in their employees. Some organisations formulate appropriate strategies to face these challenges and gain and sustain competitive advantage, whereas other organisations adopt ad hoc strategies. The following are guidelines for adopting a 'best practice' strategy for developing your employees' talent:

A: Awareness, alignment and achievements

1   Be aware that the world in which you operate is changing dramatically and that strategies have to be formulated and implemented within the context of uncertainty.

2   Develop your organisational capability to track and assess these changes, and develop talent and build knowledge to cope with these changes.

3   Recruit the talent that you need not just to meet present business needs but future business needs. Be proactive in recruiting and developing talent.

4   Develop talent at every level of your organisation.

5   Developing talent involves providing education and training on a continuous basis. Adopt the principle of continuous development in relation to developing talent.

6   Develop specialised as well as generalised talent. Focus should be on developing a mixture of talent, incorporating hard issues such as technical expertise as well as soft issues such as working in a team and being adaptable.

7   Align your talent development programmes to match your business objectives. Talent development should be matched with business objectives in order to create your organisational capabilities.

8   Use a multi-media approach to support your training and development programmes.

9   Manage diversity effectively and understand the importance of differences in national cultures. Globalisation creates a diverse workforce and with diversity is associated a variety of cultures.

10 Leverage the knowledge of your expatriates.

11 Create processes within your organisation to create and transfer knowledge.

12 Develop talent within the context of team development.

13 Formulate a strategy to retain talent. Recruiting, developing and retaining talent should constitute a composite strategy.

B: Building

1   Build a talent bank to take your business forward.

2   Create a culture of trust and collaboration.

3   Build a global outlook among your staff.

4   Build systems (intranets/extranets) to facilitate the transfer of knowledge.

5   Benchmark to adopt best practice in talent development.

C: Conviction, commitment and communication

1   Communicate your vision in order to make the talent development strategy meaningful to your staff.

2   Commit resources in good times and bad times to maintain talent development.

3   Consider providing appropriate incentives to recruit, develop and retain talent.

4   Continuous development principles should be part of your talent development strategy.

5   Coach your staff to share their tacit knowledge as they become participants in talent development programmes.

Key points

- Globalisation is here to stay.

- It impacts on the way we do business today and in the future.

- It facilitates not just the sourcing of talent but also the mobility of talent.

- It creates diversity of market place and diversity of workforce.

- It facilitates the development of talent.

SIX
Developing leadership talent – gurus' perspectives

"The best thing a leader can do is to allow each player to discover their own greatness."

BENJAMIN ZANDER

In the past few years considerable focus has been put on developing leadership talent. In the previous chapter we examined various theories of leadership developed by management writers. The question one has to ask is '**Is leadership a question of style or substance?**'

In this chapter we will explore the views of some modern writers on the themes of what leadership is and how leadership can be developed.

Warren Bennis has been described as guru of all gurus as far as leadership is concerned. In his book '*On Becoming a Leader*'[6] he presents the following basics of leadership:

- Leadership is a guiding vision.

- Leadership is a passion.

- Leadership is integrity, it involves self-knowledge, candour and maturity.

- Leadership is curiosity.

- Leadership is daring.

---

6 Bennis, Warren (1989). 'On Becoming a Leader'. Hutchison

In distinguishing leaders from managers, he wrote, 'I tend to think of the differences between leaders and managers as the differences between those who master the context and those who surrender to it. There are other differences, as well, and they are enormous and crucial:

- The manager administers; the leader innovates.

- The manager is a copy; the leader is an original.

- The manager maintains; the leader develops.

- The manager focuses on systems and structure; the leader focuses on people.

- The manager relies on control; the leader inspires trust.

- The manager has a short-range view; the leader has a long-range perspective.

- The manager asks how and when; the leader asks what and why.

- The manager has his eyes always on the bottom-line; the leader has his eye on the horizon.

- The manager imitates; the leader originates.

- The manager accepts the status quo; the leader challenges it.

- The manager is the classic good soldier; the leader is his own person.

- The manager does things right; the leader does the right thing.'

In his interview[7] Bennis said *Today's organisations are evolving into federations, networks, clusters, cross-functional teams, temporary systems, ad hoc task forces, lattices, modules, matrices – almost anything but pyramids with their obsolete top-down leadership. The new leader will encourage healthy dissent and values those followers courageous enough to say so.*

7 Brown, Crainer, Dearlove and Rodrigues (2002). 'Business Minds'.
Financial Times/Prentice Hall

This does not mark the end of leadership – but rather the need for a new, far more subtle and indirect form of influence for leaders to be effective. The new reality is that intellectual capital (brain power, knowledge and human imagination) has supplanted capital as the critical success factor; leaders will have to learn an entirely new set of skills that are not understood nor taught in our business schools, and, for all of those reasons, rarely practiced.'

Bennis also commented that 'the future has no shelf life. Future leaders will need a passion for continual learning, a refined, discerning ear for the moral and ethical consequences of their actions, and an understanding of the purpose of work and human organisations.'

He outlined four competencies that will determine the success of new leadership. They are:

1. The new leader understands and practises the power of appreciation.

2. The new leader keeps reminding people of what is important.

3. The new leader sustains and generates trust.

4. The new leader and the led are intimate allies.

Leadership views by John Kotter

Professor John Kotter of Harvard Business School has achieved international recognition as an expert on leadership in business. He writes:

'...the age-old topic of leadership has become more salient recently because of important shifts in the business environment; that leadership is no longer just the domain of the CEO or a few top managers, but it is increasingly needed in virtually all managerial jobs; that most firms today have not come close to adapting to this new reality; that successful adaptation requires changes in a few dozen managerial practices; and that such change does not come easily, but when it does come, it can serve as a powerful source of competitive advantage.

Leaders will have to learn an entirely new set of skills

Corporations are finding that even lower-level managerial, professional and technical employees sometimes need to play a leadership role in their arena.

At the same time that increased competitive intensity has been producing the need for more leadership at almost all levels in many organisations, a second set of less dramatic forces has been steadily increasing the difficulty of providing effective leadership. They are the forces of growth, diversification, globalisation, and technological development, which have been making businesses more and more complex.'

According to Kotter, the characteristics required to provide effective leadership are: motivation, personal values, abilities and skills, reputation and track-record, relationship in the firm and industry, and industry and organisational knowledge.

Organisations that do not do well in terms of developing effective leadership do so because of inadequate practices which Kotter presented as:

'They have an inadequate management, because they do not attract and retain sufficient people with leadership potential in the first place, because they do not fully develop much of the potential possessed by the employees they do not attract and retain, and because they fail to motivate (or allow) people to lead.

Their inability to attract, develop, retain and motivate sufficient leadership potential can be traced to a multitude of inadequate practices: the way they handle college recruiting, the infrequency with which they move people across divisions and functions to broaden them, the lack of coaching and support from bosses, and much more.

Most inadequate practices are created by two very powerful forces that operate inside the firms – short-term economic pressures and parochial politics, forces which influence practices both directly by shaping managerial behaviour and indirectly by influencing culture, structure and systems.

The overall syndrome is a relatively new phenomenon, the product of a changing business environment, which is demanding more and more leadership and the firm's inability (so far) to adapt successfully to that environment.'

So what should be done in order to develop leadership talent effectively? The '**best practice**' guidelines provided are:

- Let line management drive the recruiting effort.
- Target a limited number of colleges and universities that constitute a good source of future leadership and develop good relationships with them.
- Keep recruiting standards high across the entire company.
- Pay attention to leadership potential when recruiting.
- Work hard to close the sale if you want someone badly.
- Evaluate your recruiting strategy at least once a year.
- Make your organisation a great place to work.

John Kotter (1988) 'The Leadership Factor'. Harvard Business School.

Leadership by Peter Drucker

'There is no substitute for leadership. But management cannot create leaders. It can only create the conditions under which potential leadership qualities become effective; or it can stifle potential leadership'

'Leadership requires aptitude – and men who are good chief engineers or general managers are rare enough without aptitude for leadership. Leadership also requires basic attitudes. And nothing is as difficult to define, nothing as difficult to change, as basic attitudes.'[8]

Management cannot create leaders

---

8 Drucker, Peter (1955) 'The Practice of Management'. Heinemann Professional Publishing

'In the first place, leadership is not by itself good or desirable. Leadership is a means. Leadership to what end is thus the crucial question... But effective leadership doesn't depend on charisma. Dwight Eisenhower, George Marshall and Harry Truman were singularly effective leaders, yet none possessed any more charisma than a dead mackerel. Nor are there any such things as 'leadership qualities' or a 'leadership personality'. The foundation of effective leadership is thinking through the organisation's mission, defining it and establishing it, clearly and visibly. The leaders set the goals, set the priorities and maintain the standards. He makes compromises, of course; indeed effective leaders are painfully aware that they are not in control of the universe... But before accepting a compromise, the effective leader has thought through what is right and desirable. The leader's first task is to be the trumpet that sounds a clear sound.

The Japanese recognise that there are really only two demands of leadership. One is to accept that rank does not confer privileges; it entails responsibilities. The other is to acknowledge that leaders in an organisation need to impose on themselves that congruence between deeds and words, between behaviour and professed beliefs and values, that we call personal integrity.'[9]

'The higher up the monkey goes, the more of his behind he shows'.

> There are no such things as leadership quality or leadership personality

9 Drucker, Peter (1992) 'Managing For the Future'. Butterworth Heinemann

Peter Senge on leadership

Peter Senge is a guru on learning organisation. In his book 'The Fifth Discipline'[10] he expresses the following views on leadership.

Leader as designer

"Imagine that your organisation is an ocean liner, and that you are 'the leader'. What is your role?"

I have asked this question of groups of managers many times. The most common answer, not surprisingly is 'the captain'. Others say 'The navigator, setting the direction'. Still others say 'The helmsman, actually controlling the direction,' or 'the engineer down there stoking the fire, providing energy,' or 'the social director, making sure everybody's enrolled, involved and communicating'. While these are legitimate leadership roles, there is another which, in many ways, eclipses them all in importance. In essence the leaders' task is designing the learning processes. Yet, rarely does any one think of it.

The neglected leadership role is the designer of the ship. No one has a more sweeping influence than the designer. What good does it do for the captain to say, 'Turn starboard thirty degrees,' when the designer has built a rudder that will turn only to port, or which takes six hours to turn to starboard? It's fruitless to be the leader in an organisation that is poorly designed. Isn't it interesting that so few managers think of the ship's designer when they think of the leader's role?

Although 'leader as designer' is neglected today, it touches a chord that goes back thousands of years. To paraphrase Lao-tzu, the bad leader is he who people despise. The good leader is he who the people praise. The leader is he who the people say, 'we did it ourselves'.

Whereby people throughout the organisation can deal productively with the critical issues they face, and develop their mastery in the learning disciplines."

---

10 Senge, Peter M (1990). 'The Fifth Discipline'. Century Business

Tom Peters on leadership talent

In his book 'Thriving on chaos'[11] Tom Peters presents a new view of leadership at all levels.

'So now the chief job of the leader, at all levels, is to oversee the dismantling of dysfunctional old truths, and to prepare people and organisations to deal with them – to love, to develop affection for – change per se, as innovations are proposed, tested, rejected, modified and adopted.'

The guiding premise is Master paradox. *'Today's successful business leaders will be those who are most flexible of mind. An ability to embrace new ideas, routinely challenge old ones, and live with paradox will be the effective leader's premier trait.'*

'The three leadership tools for establishing direction are:

1. *Develop an inspiring vision.*

2. *Manage by example.*

3. *Practise visible management.*

Lead by empowering people. Become a compulsive listener. Cherish the people at the front-line. Delegate effectively. Bash bureaucracy.

Evaluate everyone on his or her love of change. Create a sense of urgency. Leaders must epitomise change in every action in order to create an overwhelming sense of urgency throughout the organisation.'

In commenting on 'Transforming leadership' **Peters and Waterman**[12] write:

'The transforming leader is concerned with minutiae, as well. But he is concerned with a different kind of minutiae; he is concerned with the tricks of the pedagogue, the mentor, the linguist – the more successfully to become the value shaper, the exemplar, the maker of meanings. His

---

11 Peters, Tom (1987). 'Thriving on Chaos'. Alfred A. Knopf
12 Peters, Thomas J and Waterman, Robert H. (1982). 'In Search of Excellence – Lessons from America's Best-Run Companies'. Harper & Row

job is much tougher than that of the transactional leader, for he is the true artist, the true pathfinder. After all, he is both calling forth and exemplifying the urge for transcendence that unites us all. At the same time, he exhibits almost boorish consistency over long periods of time in support of his one or two transcending values. No opportunity is too small, no form too insignificant, no audience too small.'

Noel Tichy and Mary Anne Devanna write on 'The Transformational Leader':[13]

'*The time has come to talk about how corporations, our wealth-producing institutions, can develop the type of leadership with the courage and imagination to change our corporate lifestyles. What's needed, in historian James McGregor Burn's terms, is not the old style transactional leadership but a new transformational leadership.*

Transformational leadership is about change, innovation, and entrepreneurship… this brand of leadership is a behavioural process capable of being learned and managed.'

The main task of transformational leader is to recognise the need for revitalisation, creating a new vision and institutionalising change. The main characteristics of transformational leaders are:

- They identify themselves as change agents.
- They are courageous individuals.
- They believe in people.
- They are value-driven.
- They are life long learners.
- They have the ability to deal with complexity.
- They are visionaries.

---

13 Tichy, Noel M and Devanna, Mary Anne (1986). 'The Transformational Leader', John Wiley

Steven Covey

Steven Covey, the author of 'The Seven Habits of Highly Effective People' makes the following comments on interpersonal leadership talent:

'Think win/win is the habit of interpersonal leadership. It involves the exercise of each of the unique human endowments – self-awareness, imagination, conscience, and independent will – in our relationships with others. It involves mutual learning, mutual influence, mutual benefits.

The principle of win/win is fundamental to success in all our interactions. It involves character, relationships and agreements.'

Five leadership practices common to successful leaders are highlighted:

- Challenging the process.
- Inspiring a shared vision.
- Enabling others to act.
- Modelling the way.
- Encouraging the heart.

Leadership is not only about leaders; it is also about followers

'These practices are not the private property of the leaders we studied. They are available to anyone who wants to accept the leadership challenge.

Leadership is not only about leaders; it is also about followers... Leadership is in the eye of the follower'.

Their researches indicated that the majority of us admire leaders who are honest, competent, forward-looking and inspiring.

'Wanting to lead and believing that you can lead are only the departure points on the path to leadership. Leadership is an art, a performing art. And in the art of leadership, the artist's instrument is the self. The mastery of the art of leadership comes with the mastery of the self. Ultimately, leadership development is a process of self-development.'

So what are the key messages from management gurus?

- They all emphasise the importance of effective leadership in a complex and uncertain business world.

- Leadership qualities can be acquired.

- All emphasise the importance of leadership at all levels.

- They warn us not to distinguish between managers and leaders.

- They focus on the transformational leader as opposed to transactional leadership.

- Modern organisations should be prepared to embrace transformational leadership.

- Short-term economic gains should not put pressure on corporations to take long-term views of developing transformational leadership talent.

- Leadership is about communicating vision, commitment, conviction, courage, credibility and facing challenges to create a thriving and innovative work environment.

'If you are planning for one year, grow rice.

If you are planning for 20 years grow trees.

If you are planning for centuries, grow people.'

A CHINESE PROVERB

SEVEN
Developing leadership talent: Softer approach

"Tactics are important but they do not win football matches. Players win football matches. The best teams stand out because they are teams, because the individual players have been truly integrated so that the team functions with a single spirit."

SIR ALEX FERGUSON

Leadership arises out of personal mastery. According to Bennis, Parikh and Lessem,[14] *'Alfred Sloan and Martin Luther King, although from very different walks of life, both possessed one thing in common. They had attained self-mastery, and they had developed a vision.'*

Importance of shared vision: 'I have a dream'

Bennis, Warren and Parikh go on to write, *'The visionary leader may generate new views of the future and may be a genius of synthesising and articulating them, but this makes a difference only when the vision has been successfully communicated throughout the organisation and effectively institutionalised as a guiding principle. Visionary leaders are only as powerful as the ideas they can communicate. His or her basic*

---

14 Bennis, Warren, Parikh, Jagdish, Lessem, Ronnie (1994). 'Beyond Leadership – Balancing Economics, Ethics and Ecology.' Blackwell

philosophy must be: 'We have seen what this organi-
sation can be, we understand the consequences of that
vision, and now we must act to make it so'. A vision
cannot be established in an organisation by edict, or by the
exercise of power or coercion. It is more an act of persuasion,
of creating an enthusiastic and dedicated commitment to a vision because
it is right for the times, right for the organisation, and right for the people
who are working in it.

A vision cannot be established in an organisation by edict

A vision of the future is not offered once and for all and then allowed
to fade away. It must be repeated time and again. It must be incorpo-
rated in the organisation's culture and reinforced through the strategy
and decision-making process. It must be constantly evaluated for possible
change in the light of new circumstances.'

An effective leader must be able to communicate his or her vision. This does not mean sending e-mails or memos and articulating corporate vision; to light fire in peoples' bellies vision must be articulated inter-personally. Shared vision incorporates the involvement of many individuals. A shared vision gives meaning to work and it prompts contribution and effort.

According to Peter Senge,[15] *'A vision is truly shared when you and I have a similar picture and are committed to one another having it, not just to each of us, individually, having it. When people truly share a vision they are connected, bound together by a common aspiration. Personal visions derive their power from an individual's deep caring for the vision. Shared visions derive their power from a common caring.'*

A vision of the future is not offered once and for all... It must be repeated time and again

---

15 Senge, Peter (1990). 'The Fifth Discipline – The Art and Practice of the Learning Organisation'. Century Business

Sharing vision: Extrinsic or intrinsic?

The leader needs to 'empathise' with his/her followers. He/she has to be trained in 'switching frames of reference' in order to communicate effectively.

Peter Senge (1990) cautions against purely focusing on shared visions which are extrinsic. He gives examples of organisations that focus on beating their competitors in the competitive arena. He writes, 'Such defensive goals rarely call forth the creativity and excitement of building something new. A master in the martial arts is not probably focused so much on 'defeating all others', as on his own intrinsic inner standards of 'excellence'. This does not mean that visions must be either intrinsic or extrinsic. Both types of vision can coexist. But reliance on a vision that is solely predicated on defeating an adversary can weaken an organisation long-term. A shared vision, especially one that is intrinsic, uplifts people's aspirations.'

Importance of open communication

In developing leadership talent it is very important to develop the skill of communication, not just formal communication but interpersonally.

For leadership training the Johari Window could be used to create a high degree of open and honest communication. The Johari framework facilitates communication by using what the parties involved know about themselves and others.

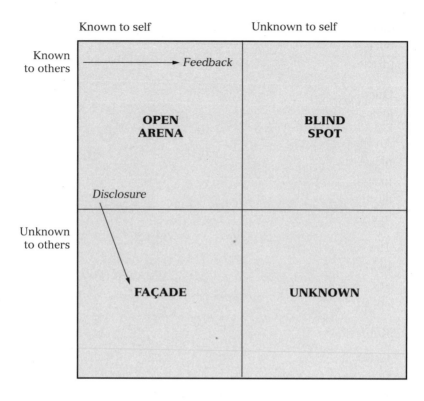

Figure 1: The Johari Window Framework of Communication

Information about an individual is represented from two perspectives, information known and unknown by self, and information known and unknown by others. Together they form the following four quadrants:

Quadrant 1. Open or public arena. This area of 'free' activity refers to behaviour known to self and known to others. This area is part of our conscious self.

Quadrant 2. The blind area or blind spot. Others can see things in ourselves of which we are unaware. When others express their views constructively of what they see this is the feedback which, if we accept what is being said, increases the area of the public arena.

Quadrant 3. Hidden arena or façade. Information known to ourselves but not revealed to others. When we reveal information about ourselves (disclosure), the area of the public arena increases.

Quadrant 4. Unknown arena. Neither the individual nor others are aware of certain behaviours.

An effective and transformational leader has to been trained to communicate openly and share information (feedback and disclosure) in order to open up and expand quadrant 1. Expansion of this quadrant will affect all other quadrants. As quadrant 1 grows larger other quadrants shrink in area.

The Blind Spot represents the dark side of the organisation reflected in hidden agendas, jobs for the boys, victimisation, intimidation, collusion and conspiracies of silence. These factors are behavioural indicators of corporate culture.

Kouzes and Posner[16] write:

'Leaders understand that unless they communicate and share information with their constituents, few will take much interest in what is going on. Unless people see and experience the effects of what they do, they won't care. When leaders share information rather than guard it, people feel included and respected. A greater two-way flow of information is created. Sharing information also lets everyone know the reasons behind decisions and the ways they are linked to shared values and common purpose. When people have the same information and understand that they are part of a community, with common values and shared interests, the results flow. Finally, everyone can sing in unison, from the same page of the same song sheet.'

An effective leader has to learn the art of feedback. He or she has to create an 'I am OK and you're OK' type of environment. This concept comes from transactional analysis and it is very important in creating a collaborative and thriving corporate culture. Opening the 'Open Arena'

---

16 Kouzes, James M and Prosner, Barry Z. (1993) 'Credibility – How Leaders Can Gain and Lose It, Why People Demand It.' Jossey-Bass Publishers

facilitates not only effective communication, but encourages creation and transfer of knowledge, which is one of the key pre-requisites of the innovative organisation.

A link must be made between corporate vision and objectives, and employee's performance objectives

Feedback is important because, in the field of communication, one has to assume that the people we communicate with are different from us – the extent of that difference depends on culture, age, gender, education, experience and so on. We can expect that any message we send may be interpreted differently from how we intended. We must, therefore, look for feedback to determine how the message was interpreted.

One aspect of feedback is **performance appraisals**.

Employees are one of the key groups of stakeholders involved in any organisation. Apart from recognising their interests and expectations from the perspective of the organisation, it is important to measure their performance to determine their effectiveness in making a contribution towards organisational objectives and success, and finding out if they have understood the corporate vision.

A link must be made between corporate vision and objectives, and employee's performance objectives. Without such a link the appraisal has no meaning and no context.

The setting up of an appraisal system involves looking at the following:

- What is expected from an individual.
- Why it is expected.
- How the outcomes are geared to organisational mission and objectives.
- How the indicators are formulated and who is involved in the measurement process.
- What the time involved is and when they should be performed.

The feedback given should address the following questions on behalf of the employees:

- What is expected of me?
- How am I doing?
- Am I on target?
- How can I improve?
- What is my reward?
- Where do I go from here?

It's not whether you win or lose, its how you play the game

The success of appraisals depends on effective feedback. To be effective feedback should be:

- Honest.
- Specific.
- It should address the main issues.
- Meaningful.
- Accurate.
- It could be acted upon.
- Followed up soon.

Trust is important. If you have not shown a genuine interest in your staff throughout the year, they are not going to take you seriously when you conduct appraisals.

Creating a thriving work environment

An effective leader has to create corporate culture that facilitates collaboration, sharing of information and knowledge, and trust. In the present climate he/she has to think about creating a family-work balance.

Many surveys and researches have indicated that helping employees to balance their **work-life balance** has become a business imperative. An organisation which is developing a workplace culture that is inclusive and encourages innovation is more likely to be able to recruit and retain talented employees. According to the new Work Foundation Report, companies will fail to attract and retain the best candidates unless they become more father-friendly. Human resources strategies have to include both parents in flexible-working and childcare policies.

A work-life balance strategy is very important in formulating a talent development strategy. An effective leadership has positively to encourage and communicate this practice. It has shown that such a strategy reduces turnover, stress related absence, encourages talent development, promotes flexibility within the work environment, encourages loyalty and has a positive impact on productivity.

Leadership and emotional intelligence

According to Daniel Goleman, emotional intelligence has direct applicability in the area of work and organisational effectiveness. Emotional intelligence is about the abilities to recognise and regulate emotions in ourselves and others. It incorporates understanding self, managing self, social awareness and managing interpersonal relationships. The two dimensions focused on are intra-personal and interpersonal intelligence.

Interpersonal intelligence is about the ability to understand and motivate other people. An effective leader has to have a high degree of interpersonal intelligence. **Intra-personal intelligence** is about the ability to transform oneself to achieve desired results.

In his article in the Harvard Business Review,[17] Goleman writes, 'Unlike IQ, which is largely genetic – it changes little from childhood – the skills of emotional intelligence can be learned at any age. It's not easy, however, growing your emotional intelligence. It takes practice and commitment. But the payoffs are well worth the investment.'

Any leadership training programme, therefore, must look at how an individual can develop and improve his emotional intelligence.

Personal mastery

Personal mastery is a difficult concept to grasp especially in the western culture. It is about an individual creating a perpetual change in our attitudes and belief systems. As Parikh[18] puts it, 'You can, at any stage in the cycle of your life be 'reborn' (psychologically). You can 'renew' yourself. Not only is this possible, but there exists the possibility of perpetual renewal in virtually every aspect of our lives through a perceptual process of rebirth. This requires a fresh look at the inner potential that each one of us possesses.'

According to Senge (1990), 'personal mastery goes beyond competence and skills, though it is grounded in competence and skills. It goes beyond spiritual unfolding or opening, although it requires spiritual growth. It means approaching one's life as a creative work, living from a creative as opposed to reactive viewpoint.'

Components of personal mastery include individual values, continuously asking and clarifying what is important and learning to see current reality more clearly. Personal mastery is about total development of self.

It incorporates developing your mental models (changing images and programmes in your mind), your interpersonal communication skills,

---

17 Daniel Goleman. 'Leadership That Gets Results'. March-April, 2000
18 Parikh, Jagdish (1991). 'Managing Your Self'. Basil Blackwell

your influencing styles. Above all it involves achieving congruence in three dimensions of your life (personal and professional):

- What you are doing.
- What you like to do.
- What you could do given the opportunity.

Developing a creative viewpoint

Dr. Gerald Kushel has written a very interesting book entitled 'The Inside Track to Successful Management'.[19] In it he shows how to practise 'effective thinking'. Effective thinkers according to Kushel know how to manage their inner and personal lives so well that the management of others falls into place, almost as a second nature.

He writes, '*Effective thinkers are excellent models. They tend to lead by example. One of them said "Values are caught, rather than taught". Without really seeming to try very hard, they add significantly to the quality of life of those who work around them.*

When they find that they have a shortcoming (and they do) they simply face up to it and then take whatever steps are necessary to remedy it, if it makes sense to do so. "I can learn anything, if I put my mind to it".'

Effective thinking is a foundation for a successful life. Kushel has studied uncommonly successful people (he calls them USPs) – people who have achieved success in three dimensions: high job performance, high level of job satisfaction and high level of satisfaction with their personal life. These people have inner calm, clarity of purpose and a sense of adventure. Effective thinking involves the following aspects of oneself:

- You are responsible for your own thoughts.
- It is more than positive thinking.

---

19 Kushel, Gerald (1998). 'The Inside Track to Successful Management.' Thorogood

- The process is results-oriented.
- Even negative thinking can sometimes be highly effective.
- It builds on conventional thinking.
- It provides for our individual differences.
- There is an effective thoughts for any situation that life dishes up.

Are you on track for effective thinking?

Self-assessment test

According to Dr. Kushel this test will sensitise you to areas you may have been neglecting.

Please circle the number that indicates your level of agreement with each statement. Scoring instructions are at the end of the instrument.

1. I quickly turn most 'problems' that come my way into 'manageable projects'.

9	8	7	6	5	4	3	2	1
AGREE								DISAGREE

2. I am a healthy sceptic, but definitely not a cynic.

9	8	7	6	5	4	3	2	1
AGREE								DISAGREE

3. I have a clear inner identity that goes far beyond my given name, my job title or even my family roles. I definitely know who I am – especially at the inner self level.

9	8	7	6	5	4	3	2	1
AGREE								DISAGREE

4. I have made the distinction between being reasonable and being realistic and I tend to be realistic more often than not.

9	8	7	6	5	4	3	2	1
AGREE								DISAGREE

5. I appreciate that anger stems from fear. Since I generally have very little to fear, I rarely get angry.

9	8	7	6	5	4	3	2	1
AGREE								DISAGREE

6. I consider myself a 'thought-chooser'. I practise pro-active thought choosing as much as it makes sense. I refuse to be an indiscriminate user or victim of any thought or series of thoughts that happen to 'come to mind'. I use every means I know of to help take charge of whatever it is that I think.

9	8	7	6	5	4	3	2	1
AGREE								DISAGREE

7. No matter what my presence of mind, I still reserve the right to think that somehow, some way 'the best is yet to come'.

9	8	7	6	5	4	3	2	1
AGREE								DISAGREE

8. I appreciate that success is a journey rather than a destination and I make it my business to enjoy the journey as much as is humanly possible, but not at the expense of others.

9	8	7	6	5	4	3	2	1
AGREE								DISAGREE

9. I understand and appreciate the value of listening to feelings and I do, when appropriate.

9	8	7	6	5	4	3	2	1
AGREE								DISAGREE

10. When appropriate, I make good use of rapid self-hypnosis to assist me in effective choosing.

9	8	7	6	5	4	3	2	1
AGREE								DISAGREE

11. I appreciate that values are caught rather than thought and try, therefore, to lead others by example.

9	8	7	6	5	4	3	2	1
AGREE								DISAGREE

12. I fully appreciate that life is much too serious not to have a sense of humour about it and I do have a sense of humour about life.

9	8	7	6	5	4	3	2	1
AGREE								DISAGREE

13. I am assertive when it makes sense to be assertive.

9	8	7	6	5	4	3	2	1
AGREE								DISAGREE

14. I tend to turn so-called 'failures' into positive 'learning experiences'.

9	8	7	6	5	4	3	2	1
AGREE								DISAGREE

15. I tend to have 'preferences', rather than absolute 'needs'.

9	8	7	6	5	4	3	2	1
AGREE								DISAGREE

16. When it comes to managing others, I realise that that takes place only by 'influence' and not by control of others. I realise that the only thing I fully control is my own thought choices, not the thought choices of others.

9	8	7	6	5	4	3	2	1
AGREE								DISAGREE

17. When making a presentation I know how to manage myself first, then my material and then the audience.

9	8	7	6	5	4	3	2	1
AGREE								DISAGREE

18. I negotiate to win/win as much as possible.

9	8	7	6	5	4	3	2	1
AGREE								DISAGREE

19. I appreciate the value of coaching and know the steps involved to coach effectively.

9	8	7	6	5	4	3	2	1
AGREE								DISAGREE

20. I know how to get close to people that are very important to me. I know when and how to trust others and myself.

9	8	7	6	5	4	3	2	1
AGREE								DISAGREE

21. I leave myself open to constructive criticisms from time-to-time. I make objective periodic self-assessments that relate to managing others. I have an action plan for improving my weaknesses.

9	8	7	6	5	4	3	2	1
AGREE								DISAGREE

22. I know how to manage my emotions and do so, when appropriate.

9	8	7	6	5	4	3	2	1
AGREE								DISAGREE

23. I am an effective risk taker. I take wise, not indiscriminate, risks, but I do take risks.

9	8	7	6	5	4	3	2	1
AGREE								DISAGREE

24. I appreciate that, in general, people tend to treat you the way that you teach them to treat you. I teach people to treat me with respect.

9	8	7	6	5	4	3	2	1
AGREE								DISAGREE

25. I appreciate that business is a game and that life is serious and I play 'the management game' to win.

9	8	7	6	5	4	3	2	1
AGREE								DISAGREE

26. I value quality over quantity, in relationships, in the things I do and in life.

9	8	7	6	5	4	3	2	1
AGREE								DISAGREE

27. I face harsh realities of life directly, grieve rapidly for them when appropriate, and then get on with my life, living it as effectively as possible, from that point on.

9	8	7	6	5	4	3	2	1
AGREE								DISAGREE

Source: 'The Inside Track to Successful Management', Gerald Kushel. Thorogood.

Scoring

If your total is between 252 and 224 you are, indeed, an effective thinker and have the tools for being an effective leader in your field.

If you scored between 223 and 112, you are currently in the middle range. You can expect to become, in a relatively short time, a highly successful leader. Take time now to review your various responses and consider the actions you should take.

Finally, if you scored 111 or less you are in the lowest third. You undoubtedly are more than a bit self-defeating, especially when it comes to job satisfaction or personal life satisfaction. Take action to review your life and your personal mastery. Remember 'the best is yet to come'.

Consider this:

'No great improvements in the lot of mankind are possible until a great change takes place in the fundamental constitution of their modes of thought.'

JOHN STUART MILL

Key points

- To become an effective leader focus on 'softer' issues that matter.

- Develop and communicate your vision.

- Incorporate your vision in the organisation culture.

- Conviction, communication and commitment are the three 'Cs' of effective leadership.

- Focus on extrinsic as well as intrinsic vision.

- Communicate openly, honestly and effectively.

- Use personal performance appraisals to embed your corporate vision.

- Help your staff to achieve work-life or work-family balance.

- Develop your emotional intelligence.

- Manage your self totally and be an effective thinker.

EIGHT
Case studies – we can do it

Talent recruitment, retention and management

"You cannot lead what you don't understand and you can't understand what you haven't done."

MYRON TRIBUS, DIRECTOR OF THE AMERICAN QUALITY AND PRODUCTIVITY INSTITUTE

The biggest challenge facing any organisation is to retain their talent. According to the website www.management-issues.com, recruitment pressures have increased despite the economic slowdown and a wave of redundancies.

They cite The Chartered Institute of Personnel and Development survey undertaken recently which states that the problem exists across all sectors and regions with more than nine out of ten of the 557 organisations surveyed experiencing difficulties.

Some organisations lose talent because they are sick of their immediate boss. Some bosses have not been trained in the softer skills of managing people. This would be one of the areas to address in developing and retaining talent.

The E-executive Issue, the newsletter published by Management Europe, reported the content of their HR 2003 conference. One of the speakers at the conference, Curt Coffman of The Gallup Organisation 'began by segmenting employees into three categories – those who are engaged, those who are not engaged, and those who are actively disengaged. As you would expect, those engaged have the most positive contribution to give an organisation. Employees who are engaged are more productive, more profitable, work more safely, and stay longer. Engaged employees emotionally engage their customers.' Those disengaged on the other hand, may be physically present, but, 'are psychologically disruptive, unhappy, and insist on sharing their unhappiness with others'. And those negatively engaged represent a significant proportion of the workforce: Gallup® found that in the UK in 2001, for example, only 17% of employees were engaged, 63% were not engaged, and 20% were actively disengaged. In Germany in 2002, the story was similar, with only 15% engaged, and 69% not engaged. And in France in the same year, only 6% of employees were found to be engaged.'

> Some organisations lose talent because they are sick of their immediate boss

Some organisations use a variety of methods to retain talent; these include:

- Laundry and car repair services.
- In-house gym or gym membership.
- Health care.
- Assistance with childcare and elderly care.
- Paid paternity leave.
- Coaching and mentoring.
- Realistic job expectations.
- Flexible working patterns.
- Fairness in employment practices.

The following are examples of some real-life organisations which are making efforts to retain and develop their talent.

Systematic

'Systematic is an independent software company that focuses on complex and critical IT solutions within information and communications systems. These systems are often mission critical, which means that there are high demands for reliability, security, user-friendliness and effectiveness. The company is based in Aarhus in Denmark.

The ability to produce quality software on time is dependent on the knowledge and commitment of our employees. We therefore, put a strong emphasis on attracting and retaining the best software engineers in the market. We must provide a stimulating and challenging workplace with active investment in the professional and personal development.'

ATTRACTING THE BEST IN THE MARKET

Potential employees are reached through various channels. The most effective method of recruitment is by word of mouth which involves employees recommending Systematic to their friends, acquaintances and fellow students. More than one out of three new employees is hired in this way. This fact is confirmed by the employee satisfaction survey undertaken in 2001 in which 93% answered positively to the question, 'I can recommend others to look for employment at Systematic'.

Our Intellectual Capital Report has also proved to be an effective marketing tool for attracting potential employees. Other methods include visits to universities, open-house invitations, assistance with teaching and examinations, participation in programmes for industrial research projects etc.

In terms of pay and conditions of employment, it is Systematic's policy to have competitive salaries, staff benefits including a pension programme and canteen, and to be very proactive towards competence development. In addition to this we have an active social club which annually arranges about 30 activities including sports, parties, outings and lectures.

From their very first day, new systems engineers are attached to a project, joining the projects on equal terms with the other team members. All new employees are allocated a tutor who supplements the professional introduction programme with pieces of good advice on practical matters.

The new employees are encouraged to make frequent use of a little notebook called 'I wonder' and write down the things they find inappropriate or miss in their introduction programme. Our Human Talent Manager currently follows up on the newly employed and has responsibility for extracting knowledge from 'I wonder'.

COMPETENCE DEVELOPMENT

'It is our ambition to be amongst the top European software companies as well as to be an attractive workplace for professional systems engineers. This ambition can only be fulfilled if we focus on all aspects of learning and training. It is the management who lay down the strategy, but it is the employees who create results and thereby value for customers and end-users.

Therefore, persistent and determined development of employee competence has high priority. We are convinced that time and money for Systematic competence development is one of the best investments in our line of business. We feel content if our employees feel that they improve on a daily basis and develop both professionally and personally.

Software development is, in itself, a difficult craft, but mission critical systems make particularly high demands on the professional competencies of the employees across development platforms, programming languages, databases, object-oriented analysis and design, communication protocols etc. In addition to this come all the soft skills needed within project management, understanding customers etc.

We want every employee to take responsibility and initiative with regard to their own competence development. We believe that the biggest effect occurs when employees are their own driving force. However, the individual plans must naturally be coordinated with the strategic needs of the company as well as the specific requirements of the project. It usually succeeds.

Every autumn, we conduct appraisals with the employees. The review is divided into four themes (1) assessment of tasks during the previous 12 months, (2) follow up on last year's success criteria and development plan, (3) determination of the development plan and success criteria for the coming year and (4) comments and good advice to the top management, to the Business Unit Director and to the Project Manager. It is our goal that all employees should have at least 75% of their individual development plan fulfilled by the following year's review.

Systematic has developed its own intranet-based competence management system, the 'Competence Universe', for recording each employee's competence profile. Each employee assesses him or herself and prepares his/her own profile. The employees may take inspiration from a predefined list of competencies, but may also add their own special capabilities. This assessment is rated on a scale from 1 to 5.

Competence development is more than merely training – a lot more. But training is an important part of Systematic competence development. Therefore, we are always extending our training activities, internally as well as externally.

All new employees go through an induction programme in which they are introduced to Systematic's culture, processes and everyday tools. During the first couple of months there is also an introduction of the various business areas and internal support functions.

It is our goal that at least a quarter of our systems engineers should be able to take on the role of a team or project leader. In cooperation with the DELTA Institute, we have developed an intensive project management course which is conducted every year (as far as this is possible) and aiming to stimulate both the left and the right side of the brain. These courses contribute to our ability to appoint internal talents to most of our management positions despite the rapid expansion.'[20]

---

20 Source: Systematic Intellectual Capital Report 2002

BT

This is an extract from BTs Annual Review and Summary Financial Statement 2003.

'Every company says that its people are its most valuable asset. That's the easy bit. But if you want to see whether or not they mean it, take a look at how much that company invests in training and development, how well managed and rewarded its people are and how they are encouraged to give their best.

Our reputation as a progressive and innovative employer not only helps us to recruit and retain an excellent workforce, it also enhances our ability to serve our customers and generate revenues and shareholder value.

During the year, we spent around £70 million on the training and development of BT people.

Because we want every single one of our 104,700 employees to be focused on delivering an excellent customer experience, a number of our training programmes tackle aspects of customer care, and 'back-to-the-floor' exercises, designed to re-familiarise senior managers with the issues that confront customer-handling staff.

And because we believe that the quality of leadership talent in the company is essential to the successful delivery of our strategy, we have put in place a number of leadership capability initiatives, ranging from programmes for newly-appointed first-time supervisors to development opportunities for our most senior managers.

We are an equal opportunities employer and want the profile of our workforce to reflect the diversity of the population as a whole. We are active in many equal opportunities and diversity organisations, and our work on gender, age, sexual orientation, race equality and disability is widely recognised. And we actively encourage a flexible approach to work/life balance. Part-time working, working from home, alternative attendance pattern, job sharing, maternity and paternity leave – all help ensure that we have access to the widest possible pool of talent.'

Volkswagen Group UK

The culture being developed at Volkswagen Group UK Ltd under the 'New Retail' banner sees employees at the centre of the corporate philosophy.

Extensive learning resources centres, a medical suite, a varied social calendar and, importantly, providing forums to elicit feedback from staff on company issues, have resulted in a highly contented workforce. This is reflected in the company's position of 13th in the recent Sunday Times '100 Best Companies to Work For' survey. It is interesting to note that 91 percent of respondents felt proud to work for Volkswagen Group UK, and nine out of ten employees believe that benefits and rewards offered by the company compare favourably with industry competitors.

Staff remuneration is excellent, with nearly three-quarters of the Milton Keynes-based workforce earning in excess of £30,000 per annum. All employees benefit from with-profit-related pay and bonuses.

Volkswagen Group (UK)'s head office is located at the edge of a picturesque lake, an ideal environment in which to enjoy treats such as free ice creams on hot summer days. The company also provided all staff, including contractors, with a free Christmas food hamper in 2003.

Holiday entitlement at the company is highly competitive, starting at 27 days each year. Maternity leave allowance is also competitive, with 18 weeks on full pay and another 22 on half pay being permitted. Company cars, a fuel allowance, a life insurance scheme and private healthcare are all offered to many staff.

The tangible benefits to those working at Volkswagen Group (UK) are many. However, major emphasis on the job satisfaction is also encouraged. Those at the vehicle importer appreciate this and five out of six employees admit they would miss the company if they were to leave.

Hilton

The Hilton operates 77 four and five star hotels within the UK and Ireland.

The Esprit Club was launched for employees in March 2002, seeking to create a culture of motivation and achievement within the organisation, and currently has 14,000 members. Esprit is a motivational tool designed to make work more enjoyable and more rewarding.

The ideas of recognition, respect and reward are key elements in the success of Esprit which encompasses a series of competitive training and development initiatives, and a rewards programme that gives colleagues a choice of benefits that suit them.

StarPoints can be earned through Hilton as rewards for achievement and guest service. Using StarPoints, colleagues can redeem a choice of benefits at a discount. Benefits include discounted hotel accommodation and food and beverage, health club membership, special rates on flights and car rental, a discount on beds, mobile phones and wines and spirits. Colleagues also have the option of donating their StarPoints to the Hilton charity, the Hilton in the Community Foundation.

Elevator is Hilton's fast track programme, which over the course of 18 months puts individuals through intensive training in different departments. Upon completing the course, graduates move into senior positions in Hilton hotels all around the world. The Hilton University was set up in September 2001 to provide Hilton colleagues with learning and education opportunities to develop their careers. This is based online and enables those with ambition to get ahead by offering career progression, training and personal development.

Premier Class is a 9-month management development programme for senior managers in the business, which focuses on developing key management skills needed to drive personnel and business performance in their hotel. The programme covers a variety of topics including Managing People and Improving Quality.

The Hilton has policies in place that prioritize environmental issues on a large scale and adhere to all environmental legislation on a day-to-day basis. All staff and outside contractors are also encouraged to take responsibility for environmental issues. The charitable work undertaken by Hilton last year raised approximately £1 million internationally; some of the work they were involved with was to support communities who were devastated by floods in central Europe in 2002. An insurance scheme and private healthcare are all offered to many staff.

. . . .

Eversheds

Eversheds is one of the largest law firms in the world, with an annual turnover of over £250m. The firm acts for more FTSE 100 companies than any other and offers businesses the full range of legal services.

More than 4,000 people work in Eversheds' network of international offices, around half of whom are lawyers.

'Straightforward, enterprising, effective – we use these words to describe our approach to both people and clients. We simplify rather than complicate and we believe in finding a better way.

One of the firm's key objectives is to attract and retain the best people. Each year, Eversheds invest approximately £4m in training. The Attracting and Retaining Talent (ART) group meets regularly to discuss issues that are key to the firm being an employer of choice – and Eversheds' enlightened approach to career management, remuneration and flexibility in the workplace is paying off.

Eversheds was rated by the Sunday Times as one of the UK's top '100 Best Companies to Work For', and by The Times as one of the UK's top 100 graduate employers.

Eversheds is serious about developing its people. The firm offers a career structure for lawyers and is about to roll-out The Career Pathways scheme (career development for non-lawyers). Training comes in many forms – coaching, formal courses and on the job training and mentoring in the workplace.

Eversheds' flexible working scheme Lifestyle, was recently launched offering all staff a range of flexible working choices, including part-time working, job share, career breaks, sabbatical breaks, remote working and the innovative self-rostered team option.

We are about to launch a voluntary benefits package, incorporating a range of discounted products, childcare vouchers and a PC lease plan scheme – the latter two making the most of government tax and national insurance breaks.

Other benefits include a personal pension scheme, private medical insurance, life assurance, income protection cover, flexible holiday plan, generous maternity and paternity benefits, and subsidised canteens, to name a but a few.

Eversheds is committed to endeavouring to be a good corporate citizen in relation to both the people who work here and the communities that we serve. This commitment has been demonstrated to date through an expanding programme of measures designed to emphasise corporate social responsibility and pro bono activities.'

Unilever UK

Unilever produced the first branded laundry soap way back in 1885 as Lever Brothers. A leading consumer goods manufacturer, they produce brands such as Persil and Flora and bring in sales in the UK worth £2.5bn, employing 12,000 staff over 27 sites.

Believing that its people are the highest priority and central to the success of the company, Unilever invests up to £20,000 per year in the training of highly talented graduates and provide generous maternity benefits – 40 weeks at full pay after just one year of service. Subsidised gym membership and crèche facilities are also available. Believing that a satisfied and motivated workforce comes from being able to strike the balance between work and home, Unilever UK are sympathetic to outside demands.

Communications between staff members are regarded as vital and are preserved by consultation groups, team meetings and the production of their own staff magazine, keeping them informed and in touch with current news at other Unilever locations.

Such ease of communication enhances a creative culture generating a range of ideas that are in keeping with the diversity of staff members.

The three pillars of Unilever's sustainable development policy are; Agriculture, Water Management and Fisheries, with real commitment to maintaining the highest possible standards.

Unilever UK was included in the Sunday Times list of the '*100 Best Companies to Work For*', whilst also coming 4th in The Giving List, published by The Guardian. As a member of the PerCent Club which is a voluntary benchmark to measure the contributions made by companies, Unilever UK are a key contributor to corporate community investment in the UK. In 2002, the value of Unilever UK's community contributions, measured using the London Benchmarking Group model, was over £9 million.

Unilever UK is a long-standing and committed supporter of the arts, involved with both high profile commitments, such as The Unilever Series, a 5 year commission enabling Tate Modern to provide a new work of art each year, free to the public, but also heavily supporting the development of young talent, through the Unilever House Art Collection.

Unilever UK is a member of BitC, with senior executives participating in key Leadership Teams. Local sites across the UK have strong links with their surrounding schools, and the number of employees and number of partners are increasing.

. . . .

Asda

Asda, Britain's third biggest supermarket chain, has experienced such rapid expansion that they have created 35,000 new jobs over the last 5 years and now employs around 130,000 people over 259 sites.

First formed in 1965 by a group of Yorkshire farmers, the company has been through considerable turmoil since. During the 1980's new management teams were brought in to re-develop the company after a near bankruptcy. Recently Asda became part of Wal-Mart, creating yet more opportunities for expansion.

Some 75% of staff (or 'colleagues' as ASDA calls them) work part-time, and therefore flexibility is high on the agenda whether you work on the shop floor or at managerial level. Schemes such as shift-swap, job-shares, school-starter leave, Benidorm Leave (for over 50's extended winter breaks) or Grandparents' Leave enable colleagues – whatever their age or circumstances to find a good work/life balance.

ASDA also acknowledges the difficulty and the expense that childcare arrangements can present and offer discount schemes to help working parents.

Extended holidays are available for special occasions, and even career breaks for those that have worked for Asda for at least 3 years. The flexible approach extends beyond the needs of the workforce and in line with the changing requirements of competitive and consumer trends.

Each of Asda's sites reflects the diversity of its staff members with appropriate bi-lingual signs, prayer rooms, and holiday leave for non-Christian religious festivals.

Staff are rewarded for excellent service with point schemes than can be redeemed against goods or services. In this way staff know that they are valued and remain motivated by such recognition.

Similarly ASDA operates one of the UK's biggest colleague share ownership schemes and believes passionately in the motivational benefits of giving colleagues a stake in the business.

Asda has also developed environmental programmes whereby each new development acquired is landscaped to minimise environmental damage. Their ethos also includes regular charity work and has raised money for both Children in Need and Breast Cancer Care.

Microsoft

Microsoft Ltd employ 1,595 staff over 3 sites in the UK with last year's global sales worth £17bn. It has a people vision of 'creating an environment where great people can do their best work and be on a path to realise their full potential'.

The resulting environment that the strategy has driven, has led to Microsoft in the UK being voted the number one of '100 Best Companies to Work For' by the Sunday Times, they also won the award for Giving Something Back. Last year Microsoft gave a very generous 9.58% pre-tax profits to charity, involving employees in innovative schemes such as donating 10p to the NSPCC everytime an employee left work before 5.30pm. Microsoft also match funds up to the value of £7,500 per employee and has formed links with Age Concern and Ability Net.

Microsoft have a great two way deal with their employees, this extends to the staff not just in terms of their salary, where 88% of staff earn over £30,000 per annum, but to perks such as free private healthcare for staff and family, 4 months sabbatical after 4 years service and for staff based in Reading, an on-site alternative health care centre for staff to pop in for reflexology treatment, and subsidised outings to shows or trips abroad. In return the employees continue to deliver great business results for the company as well as for their customers.

The working environment has been very carefully planned to cater for different tastes. The Reading campus is built around a lake, and staff can enjoy both picnic lunches and free ice creams or make use of the variety of on-site restaurants and X-Box games terminals.

Staff can arrange flexible working hours, and staying late is not encouraged. This is definitely a culture where employees are valued and engagement with their work is a high priority.

Staff are provided with state of the art equipment necessary to fulfil their roles with both ease and flexibility. The offices are completely wireless, and ADSL connections are provided at home for all staff along with Tablet PCs and smart phones, enabling staff to focus on doing what they do best every day!

Bettys & Taylors of Harrogate

Bettys & Taylors is a family business with a family atmosphere. There are five Bettys Café Tea Rooms across Yorkshire – in Harrogate, York, Northallerton and Ilkley – a craft bakery where over 600 breads, cakes, pastries and chocolates are made by hand, and a tea and coffee factory where all the Taylors of Harrogate's teas and coffees are blended and packed.

From the moment people join the business; they are made to feel part of the family. The current chairman and great-nephew of Bettys' founder personally welcomes all new starters with a memorable 'Induction Day' when they are given a snapshot of Bettys & Taylors with a tour around the business.

Everyone who contributes to the business's success shares in it with all members of staff benefiting from a generous quarterly bonus scheme. They are also able to buy or sell up to one week's holiday, meals are provided free (with plenty of tea and cakes!), and, on their birthday, everyone receives a special 'Birthday Voucher' so that they can treat themselves to a present from Bettys. Training at Bettys Cookery School and externally helps staff to grow and develop while working for the business, with job sharing and sabbaticals on offer to help those in need of more flexible working conditions.

The real testament to the success of any of these initiatives is the reaction of staff themselves. More than 100 members of staff celebrated a 'long service anniversary' last year alone, with many having spent more than 20 years with the business.

This caring, sharing approach extends beyond staff to the communities in which, and with which, Bettys & Taylors trade. Each year, over £30,000 is raised for eight local charities democratically chosen by staff, local schoolchildren are given the chance to learn new skills and put them into practice at Bettys Cookery School, and the business donates a minimum of £10,000 to Oxfam's tree planting and community work in tea and coffee producing communities overseas.

For all these reasons, Bettys & Taylors featured in the top 20 of the Sunday Times '100 Best Companies to Work For' list for the second year running, with over 80 percent of staff saying that they felt proud to be a part of the business – and 86 percent admitting that they laugh a lot at work!

The above cases range from manufacturing to software to professional and hospitality sectors. Recruiting, retaining and developing talent is the main challenge for all types and size of organisations.

Lessons to be learned from these cases

- Knowledge and commitment of people matter.
- Provide a stimulating and challenging workplace.
- Invest in talent development.
- Align talent development strategies with business goals.
- Focus on all aspects of talent development.
- Let employees take full responsibility for their own competence development.
- Competence development is more than merely training.
- Create a reputation of being a progressive and innovative employer.
- Respect your staff and recognise their contribution.
- Be flexible in your approach to motivating and retaining your talent.
- Practise open communication.

Reading list and useful websites

Reading list: Knowledge shared is knowledge gained

- Bennis, Warren (1989). *'On Becoming a Leader'*. Hutchison Books Ltd.

- Bennis, Nanus (1985). *'The Strategies for Taking Charge'*. Harper & Row.

- Brown, Crainer, Dearlove, Rodrigues (2002). *'Business Minds'*. Financial Times/Prentice Hall.

- Covey, Stephen R (1992). *'The Seven Habits of Highly Effective People'*. Simon & Schuster.

- Drucker (1954). *'The Practice of Management'*. Butterworth-Heinemann.

- Goleman, D (1995). *'Emotional Intelligence'*. Bantam Books.

- Gilley, Kay (1997). *'Leading from the Heart'*. Butterworth-Heinemann.

- Harrison, Rosemary (1993). *'Human Resources Management'*. Addison-Wesley.

- Johnson, M. (2000). *'Winning The People War'*. Financial Times/ Prentice Hall.

- Kermally, Sultan (1996). *'Total Management Thinking'*. Butterworth-Heinemann.

- Kermally, Sultan (1997). *'Managing Performance'*. Butterworth-Heinemann.

- Kermally, Sultan (2002). *'Effective Knowledge Management'*. John Wiley.

- Kushel, Gerald (1998). *'The Inside Track to Successful Management'* Thorogood.

- Kotter, John P (1988) *'The Leadership Factor'*. The Free Press

- Kouzes, Posner (1990). *'The Leadership Challenge'*. Josey-Bass Publishers.

- Kouzes, Posner (1993). *'Credibility'*. Jossey-Bass.

- Landsberg, Max (1997). *'The Tao of Coaching'*. Harper Collins Business.

- Parikh, J (1991). *'Managing You: Management by Detached Involvement'*. Basil Blackwell.

- Senge, Peter M. (1990) *'The Fifth Discipline'*. Century Business.

- Spencer & Spencer (1993). *'Competence at Work'*. John Wiley.

- Stonehouse, Hamill, Campbell, Purdie (2000). *'Global and Transnational Business'*. John Wiley.

- Tichy, Devanna (1986). *'The Transformational Leader'*. John Wiley.

- Tichy, Sherman (1994). *'Control Your Destiny or Someone Will'*. Harper Business.

- Whiteley, Philip (2002). *'People Express'*. Capstone Publishing.

Useful websites

- www.management-issues.com.

- www.onrec.com

- www.strategy-business.com

- www.pwcglobal.com

- www.managementfirst.com

- www.parentsatwork.org.uk

- www.hrmguide.co.uk

- www.mckinseyquarterly.com

Thorogood publishing

Thorogood publishes a wide range of books, reports, special briefings and psychometric tests. Listed below is a selection of key titles.

Desktop Guides

The marketing strategy desktop guide	*Norton Paley* • £16.99
The sales manager's desktop guide	*Mike Gale and Julian Clay* • £16.99
The company director's desktop guide	*David Martin* • £16.99
The credit controller's desktop guide	*Roger Mason* • £16.99
The company secretary's desktop guide	*Roger Mason* • £16.99
The finance and accountancy desktop guide	*Ralph Tiffin* • £16.99
The commercial engineer's desktop guide	*Tim Boyce* • £16.99
The training manager's desktop guide	*Eddie Davies* • £16.99
The PR practitioner's desktop guide	*Caroline Black* • £16.99
Win new business – the desktop guide	*Susan Croft* • £16.99

Masters in Management

Mastering business planning and strategy	*Paul Elkin* • £14.99
Mastering financial management	*Stephen Brookson* • £14.99
Mastering leadership	*Michael Williams* • £14.99
Mastering negotiations	*Eric Evans* • £14.99
Mastering people management	*Mark Thomas* • £14.99
Mastering personal and interpersonal skills	*Peter Haddon* • £14.99
Mastering project management	*Cathy Lake* • £14.99
Mastering marketing	*Ian Ruskin-Brown* • £16.99

Business Action Pocketbooks

Edited by David Irwin

Building your business pocketbook	£6.99
Developing yourself and your staff pocketbook	£6.99
Finance and profitability pocketbook	£6.99
Managing and employing people pocketbook	£6.99
Sales and marketing pocketbook	£6.99
Managing projects and operations pocketbook	£6.99
Effective business communications pocketbook	£6.99
PR techniques that work	*Edited by Jim Dunn* • £6.99

Other titles

The John Adair handbook of management and leadership	*Edited by Neil Thomas* • £24.99
The pension trustee's handbook (3rd edition)	*Robin Ellison* • £25
Boost your company's profits	*Barrie Pearson* • £12.99
Negotiate to succeed	*Julie Lewthwaite* • £12.99
The management tool kit	*Sultan Kermally* • £10.99
Working smarter	*Graham Roberts-Phelps* • £14.99
Test your management skills	*Michael Williams* • £15.99
The art of headless chicken management	*Elly Brewer and Mark Edwards* • £6.99
EMU challenge and change – the implications for business	*John Atkin* • £11.99
Everything you need for an NVQ in management	*Julie Lewthwaite* • £22.99
Customer relationship management	*Graham Roberts-Phelps* • £14.99
Sales management and organisation	*Peter Green* • £10.99
Telephone tactics	*Graham Roberts-Phelps* • £10.99
Companies don't succeed people do!	*Graham Roberts-Phelps* • £12.99

Inspiring leadership	*John Adair* • £15.99
The book of ME	*Barrie Pearson and Neil Thomas* • £14.99
The complete guide to debt recovery	*Roger Mason* • £12.99
Janner's complete speechmaker	*Greville Janner* • £10.99
Gurus on business strategy	*Tony Grundy* • £14.99
Dynamic practice development	*Kim Tasso* • £19.99
Successful selling solutions	*Julian Clay* • £12.99
High performance consulting skills	*Mark Thomas* • £14.99
The concise Adair on leadership	*edited by Neil Thomas* • £9.99
The inside track to successful management	*Gerry Kushel* • £12.99
The concise time management and personal development	*John Adair and Melanie Allen* • £9.99
Gurus on marketing	*Sultan Kermally* • £14.99
The concise Adair on communication and presentation skills	*edited by Neil Thomas* • £9.99
The dictionary of colour	*Ian Paterson* • £19.99

Thorogood also has an extensive range of reports and special briefings which are written specifically for professionals wanting expert information.

For a full listing of all Thorogood publications, or to order any title, please call Thorogood Customer Services on 020 7749 4748 or fax on 020 7729 6110. Alternatively view our website at www.thorogood.ws.

BUSINESS SEMINARS

Focused on developing your potential

Falconbury, sister company to Thorogood publishing, brings together the leading experts from all areas of management and strategic development to provide you with a comprehensive portfolio of action-centred training and learning.

We understand everything managers and leaders need to **be, know and do** to succeed in today's commercial environment. Each product addresses a different technical or personal development need that will encourage growth and increase your potential for success.

- Practical public training programmes

- Tailored in-company training

- Coaching

- Mentoring

- Topical business seminars

- Trainer bureau/bank

- Adair Leadership Foundation

The most valuable resource in any organisation is its people; it is essential that you invest in the development of your management and leadership skills to ensure your team fulfil their potential. Investment into both personal and professional development has been proven to provide an outstanding ROI through increased productivity in both you and your team. Ultimately leading to a dramatic impact on the bottom line.

With this in mind Falconbury have developed a comprehensive portfolio of training programmes to enable managers of all levels to develop their skills in leadership, communications, finance, people management, change management and all areas vital to achieving success in today's commercial environment.

What Falconbury can offer you?

- Practical applied methodology with a proven results
- Extensive bank of experienced trainers
- Limited attendees to ensure one-to-one guidance
- Up to the minute thinking on management and leadership techniques
- Interactive training
- Balanced mix of theoretical and practical learning
- Learner-centred training
- Excellent cost/quality ratio

Falconbury In-Company Training

Falconbury are aware that a public programme may not be the solution to leadership and management issues arising in your firm. Involving only attendees from your organisation and tailoring the programme to focus on the current challenges you face individually and as a business may be more appropriate. With this in mind we have brought together our most motivated and forward thinking trainers to deliver tailored in-company programmes developed specifically around the needs within your organisation.

All our trainers have a practical commercial background and highly refined people skills. During the course of the programme they act as facilitator, trainer and mentor, adapting their style to ensure that each individual benefits equally from their knowledge to develop new skills.

Falconbury works with each organisation to develop a programme of training that fits your needs, this can incorporate not only traditional classroom style learning but also involve our coaching and mentoring service or advise on the development of internal mentoring programmes.

Mentoring

Falconbury delivers a world class, individual mentoring service for senior executives and entrepreneurs. The purpose is to accelerate corporate success dramatically and to enhance personal development.

Mentoring involves formulating winning strategies, setting goals, monitoring achievements and motivating the whole team whilst achieving a much improved work life balance.

The issues are addressed at regular meetings, with telephone discussions in between. Sometimes, an unexpected issue will require an additional meeting at short notice.

Coaching

Developing and achieving your personal objectives in the workplace is becoming increasingly difficult in today's constantly changing environment. Additionally, as a manager or leader, you are responsible for guiding colleagues towards the realisation of their goals. Sometimes it is easy to lose focus on your short and long-term aims.

Falconbury's one-to-one coaching draws out individual potential by raising self-awareness and understanding, facilitating the learning and performance development that creates excellent managers and leaders. It builds renewed self-confidence and a strong sense of 'can-do' competence, contributing significant benefit to the organisation. Enabling you to focus your energy on developing your potential and that of your colleagues.

For more information on all our services please contact Falconbury on 020 7729 6677 or visit the website at: www.falconbury.co.uk